Transcribed by Diane Narlock
Edited by Brad Shirley
Cover Image: Copyright © www.crestock.com

Living in the Favor of God

A Study of the Beatitudes

Dr. Leonard Gardner

2010

Living in the Favor of God

Contents

Chapter 1

Foundations of God's Favor

The passage of Scripture found in Matthew Chapters 5, 6 and 7 is commonly referred to as Jesus' "Sermon on the Mount," and it consists primarily of an introduction to the principles of the Kingdom of God. The introductory passage of the "Sermon on the Mount" is often referred to as "The Beatitudes" and we could also call them the "foundations of God's favor" as we learn about living in the favor of God. This teaching contains eight important principles, and we can rightly refer to the Beatitudes as "the preamble to the constitution of the Kingdom of God." Therefore, it is important to grasp these eight principles in order to understand the Kingdom of God in its fullness. In this book, I pray that the Holy Spirit will help us to understand precisely the powerful truths that Jesus communicated in the Beatitudes.

Immediately preceding this passage, Matthew 4:23-25 states, "And Jesus went about all Galilee, teaching in their synagogues, and preaching the gospel of the kingdom...and healing all manner of sicknesses and all manner of disease among the people. And his fame went throughout all Syria; and they brought unto him all sick people that were taken with divers diseases and torments, and those which were possessed with devils, and those which were lunatick, and those that had the palsy; and he healed them. And there followed him great multitudes of people from Galilee, and from Decapolis, and from Jerusalem, and from Judaea, and from beyond Jordan." Please note the first part of verse 25, which declares, "...there followed him great multitudes of people." The account continues in Matthew 5:1, which states, "And seeing the multitudes, he went up into a mountain and when he was set, his disciples came unto him."

Multitudes and Miracles

It is significant to note that, when Jesus ministered in the miraculous power of God, large multitudes followed Him. (Matthew 4:25) However, Matthew Chapters 5 through 7 describe a time when Jesus, in the perfect will of the Father, drew away from the multitudes and went into a high mountain to teach and unveil the great truths of the Kingdom of God. Matthew 5:1 declares that when Jesus went up the mountain, His disciples (not the multitudes) came to Him. From this passage, we learn that *multitudes pursue miracles, but disciples pursue Him*. That is a very significant truth for us to embrace. I wholeheartedly believe in miracles, and I rejoice to see God perform His miraculous works in peoples' lives. I have been privileged to witness miracles on a number of occasions throughout my life and ministry. However, I have learned that *miracles are not to be pursued. Miracles are to be experienced. Jesus is to be pursued.* Jesus' disciples pursued *Him*, but the multitudes pursued the *miracles*. How can we define a "disciple?" A disciple is not limited to one of the original twelve men who were chosen to follow Jesus. A disciple is any believer who wants more of Him, wants to hear and obey more of what He has to say, and wants to draw closer to Him. Matthew 5 illustrates the fact that the disciples had to <u>do</u> something to get to Him; they had to put forth effort. They had to make a commitment. They had to leave the crowd behind and climb a mountain!

Following Jesus

If you make up your mind that you're going to walk with Jesus and He is going to have priority in your life, you may find that the crowd's not always with you. If you have a deep desire to be a true disciple ("disciplined one") and follower of Jesus Christ, I believe that you must have a passion to pursue Him.

Our call is to follow Jesus. If we are following Him, He will tell us *what* we are to do *when* we need to know it. He doesn't reveal such things simply to satisfy our curiosity. He reveals it to show us the next step that we need to take as we follow Him. We need to make Jesus the center of our focus and desire. We are following *Him*! As we do so, He will unveil to us what we need to know, when we need to know it. So it was with the people who had gathered with Jesus that day on the mountain.

Matthew 5:2 states that Jesus sat down and "opened his mouth." He was about to reveal some truths that would be at the very foundation of their walk (and ours) from that day forward. There is a reason that "The Beatitudes" are so well known and so often quoted. The truths that Jesus revealed here are so important that we can neither truly experience His favor nor fulfill our divinely ordained purpose unless we embrace, internalize, and apply these truths to our lives.

Blessed Are...

Over the course of the pages of this book, I invite you to take your Bible and go with me "to the mountain." Together, let's sit at the feet of Jesus as He opens His mouth. Let us ask Him, by the power of His Holy Spirit, to speak to our spirits and teach us the principles that will bring us to that appointed place of fulfillment and fruitfulness in Him.

Jesus taught eight important principles in the Beatitudes. Each verse in Matthew 5:3-11 begins with the same word - "blessed." If we study this passage carefully, we will find that verses 10 and 11 work together to address a single principle while verses 3 through 9 each address a different principle, giving us a total of eight principles.

The Greek word translated "blessed" in this passage is *makarios*, which means "to be supremely fortunate; to be well off; to be *favored* by God; to be made happy and fulfilled by God." I believe the Lord wants us to be joyful, favored, fulfilled people, and as we obey His Word, that's exactly what transpires in our lives. If we are not in that condition, it is often because we are lacking in our understanding or application of the Word of God. (Hosea 4:6) Jesus effectively was saying to the people, "I want you to be favored, fulfilled, and blessed, and I will tell you how to experience that kind of lifestyle."

Condition and Provision

As we examine each of the eight principles, we will find that Jesus utilized a common structure to teach each principle. This structure could be called "the condition and the provision."

For example, Matthew 5:3 states, "Blessed are the poor in spirit; for theirs is the Kingdom of Heaven (Kingdom of God)." Jesus is saying that we are blessed, very fortunate and favored, when we are poor in spirit. That is the _condition_ - being "poor in spirit." The next phrase contains the _provision_ - "for theirs is the Kingdom of Heaven (Kingdom of God)." Therefore, satisfying the _condition_ of being "poor in spirit" yields the _provision_ of the Kingdom of Heaven (Kingdom of God). Using this structure, we can summarize the eight principles as follows.

1. You are blessed when you are poor in spirit (condition); yours is the Kingdom of God (provision). _Matthew 5:3_

2. You are blessed when you mourn (condition); you will be comforted (provision). _Matthew 5:4_

3. You are blessed when you are meek (condition); you shall inherit the earth (provision). _Matthew 5:5_

4. You are blessed when you hunger and thirst after righteousness (condition); you shall be filled (provision). _Matthew 5:6_

5. You are blessed when you are merciful (condition); you shall obtain mercy (provision). _Matthew 5:7_

6. You are blessed when you are pure in heart (condition); you shall see God (provision). _Matthew 5:8_

7. You are blessed when you are a peacemaker (condition); you shall be called the children of God (provision).

Matthew 5:9

8. You are blessed when you are persecuted for righteousness' sake (condition); yours is the Kingdom of God (provision). *Matthew 5:10-11*

The provisions mentioned in each of the eight principles are obviously desirable. Jesus wants us to have them, and I believe most people want them. We desire that the Kingdom of God be manifest in and through us. We desire to be comforted, to inherit the earth, to be filled, to obtain mercy, to see God, and to be called the children of God. Jesus clearly laid out these provisions to us, but each provision comes with a condition which first must be satisfied.

Fulfilling the Conditions

What are the conditions? We must be poor in spirit. We must mourn. We must be meek. We must hunger and thirst after righteousness. We must be merciful. We must be pure in heart. We must be a peacemaker. We must be persecuted for righteousness sake. What do these things really mean to us in our daily lives, and how do we satisfy these conditions?

We must realize that in identifying these conditions, Jesus was not speaking of our human character and/or personality. Each of us has a uniquely different human nature. For example, some people are meeker than other people. Some tend to be peacemakers, while others seem to find, cause, or enjoy conflict! Some tend to be purer in heart, while others are quite the opposite.

When the Beatitudes are interpreted (incorrectly) from a human perspective, they can cause people to think that they cannot possibly fulfill the conditions for the blessing. For example, because we may not be a "meek" person by nature, we may feel that we simply cannot meet Jesus' conditions. Some Christians have struggled with things like this for years and consequently have given up in frustration, thinking, "I can never become like that." However, we must understand that we cannot *make* ourselves "be" any of these things or fulfill these conditions through human resolve or willpower alone.

As we study each of these principles individually, we will learn that Jesus is effectively saying *the Holy Spirit has been sent to earth with a mission and purpose to accomplish in the hearts of disciples of Jesus Christ that which will produce the results of the provision of God.* We are not referring to behavior modification but rather character transformation. Therefore, if we don't recognize the Holy Spirit working in us, we will fail to yield and cooperate with Him, which will hinder the progress of His work in transforming our character.

Recognizing the Work of the Holy Spirit in Us

Jesus taught these principles so that we will recognize:

- <u>what</u> the Holy Spirit is doing in us,
- the <u>reason</u> He is doing it (so we can be blessed), and
- our responsibility (that we must yield to His working).

Again, God desires good for us. He wants to bless our

lives, but the principles of the kingdom are such that in order to receive the blessings, we must satisfy the conditions.

Jesus reminds us that when the Holy Spirit comes to us and begins to "tamper" with our lives, we are favored. We are favored because the Spirit's work in our lives will produce a *condition* that will result in the manifestation of a *provision* of God. For example, Matthew 5:6 speaks of being filled. Everyone desires to be filled, but we don't become filled simply by desiring it. Being filled is the *provision*. Since we must satisfy the *condition* in order to receive the *provision,* we cannot bypass the condition and indirectly receive the provision. Therefore, the *provision* to be filled will only be experienced when the *condition* to be hungry is satisfied. So what does the Holy Spirit do? He works in our lives to make us hungry and thirsty for righteousness. We cannot make ourselves hungry for God. The Holy Spirit must be invited to work in our hearts, and as He does, He'll create that condition (hunger), which opens the windows of heaven and allows God to fill us.

As we study the Beatitudes, we will see it is God's desire for us to be blessed and highly favored!

Chapter 2

Blessed are the Poor in Spirit

You are highly favored, fortunate, and blessed when you are poor in spirit because the Kingdom of Heaven will be yours!

The *provision* in this first principle is referred to by Jesus as "the Kingdom of God." Please don't be confused by the fact that Matthew uses the term "Kingdom of Heaven" in all but three references to the kingdom in his gospel. Matthew was a Jew, and he wrote his gospel from a Jewish perspective, including using many references to the prophecies in the Hebrew Scriptures (Old Testament) which spoke of the coming Messiah. In Matthew's day, Jews were very reluctant to use the word "God" out of a sense of reverence. They were conscious of the commandment which spoke of using the Lord's name in vain, so they would often substitute the word "Heaven" for "God." However, parallel scripture passages in the other gospels (Mark, Luke, John) use the word "God." The Kingdom of God is a very key thought in the teachings of Jesus. He began His earthly ministry teaching the Kingdom of God and He ended His earthly ministry (Acts Chapter 1) teaching the Kingdom of God. That phrase occurs one hundred four times in the synoptic gospels (Matthew, Mark, and Luke), and ninety-one times in the gospel of John. Therefore, the phrase "the Kingdom of God" appears almost two hundred times in the four gospels!

The Kingdom of God

In this book, we cannot explore in great depth the subject of the Kingdom of God. However, I believe every Christian that is established in the Lord, and desires to walk closer with Him and be used by Him, needs to understand the Kingdom of God. Otherwise, we will have great difficulty interpreting the teachings of Jesus. Therefore, let us briefly discuss the Kingdom of God as we prepare to move forward in our study of the Beatitudes.

Life has two domains. There is a visible world and an invisible world. Each of these worlds is ruled by certain principles and laws, because God is a God of order. The visible world is subject to the invisible world. We are so conscious of the visible world that we think of it as the predominant domain, but it is not so. The invisible world is the predominant domain. Revelation 11:15 declares, "The kingdoms of this world shall become the kingdoms of our Lord and His Christ." In other words, the invisible world will swallow up the visible world one day. The visible world we see every day is a very small part of what God has created. We are familiar with many of the laws in the visible world. We understand the law of gravity. We understand the laws of physics, force, leverage, etc. We further understand that if we cooperate with those laws they will be a blessing to us; they will help us. If we oppose those laws, they will hurt us because the law of sowing produces reaping. There is a cause and effect to the things that we do in the visible world.

It is similar in the invisible world (the Kingdom of God). There are principles that are active in the invisible world - "laws" if you will. Certain things that we do will produce certain results. However, the Kingdom of God, as introduced and taught by Jesus, is neither a time nor a place. It is rather a quality of life into which we enter when are born again. We enter into this dimension that has existed all along but suddenly becomes ours, and we begin to function and operate in it. We do not cease to operate in the visible world, but we begin to operate also in the invisible world, and the great provisions of God begin to come to pass. If I were to define the phrase "The Kingdom of God" in very simple terms, I would call it "the government of God." When God's sovereignty rules (governs) one's heart, mind, and will, and when one is walking in complete harmony with His Word and His purpose, certain things will result. These principles can be learned, applied, and practiced, and Jesus addressed them in the Sermon on the Mount. He said "Seek ye first the Kingdom of God and His righteousness, and all these things shall be added unto you." (Matthew 6:33) He placed great importance on the Kingdom of God. He said if you're seeking after other things, you are missing the mark because seeking the Kingdom of God will produce these things. Therefore He drew attention to the Kingdom of God.

When Jesus said that the Kingdom of God is ours, He was speaking of His complete provision. Everything that He has available to us becomes ours under His government - blessings, wholeness, eternal life, abundant life, strength, might, peace, power, mercy, grace, love, and on and on. These are the things for which our hearts long and after which we seek, the things of the Kingdom of God.

Poor in Spirit

The Holy Spirit is going to work in our lives to bring us to the point that we are "poor in spirit." The reason? So the fullness of the Kingdom of God will be experienced in our lives. Jesus said if you are "poor in spirit," then yours is the Kingdom of God.

When Jesus used the term "poor in spirit," He was not speaking of material poverty because that would be inconsistent with other Scripture. Jesus always taught His Word consistently and never taught anything which was contradictory to anything else He taught or did. He was not teaching that it is a blessing to be materially poor. If that were the case, why would Scripture encourage us to give unto the poor? If the poor are already blessed (simply because they are poor), then when we give to them, we would be making them less poor and therefore less blessed!

Obviously, we can conclude that Jesus was not talking about material blessings. We are so materially minded that we immediately interpret things in that manner. Jesus was not saying blessed are the poor in body, the poor in mind, or the poor in material possessions. He was specifically speaking of the "poor in spirit." The spirit is one part of our trichotomous (spirit/soul/body) being. The spirit is the central part, the person we actually are. Again, Jesus said we are blessed if we are poor in spirit.

There are two different Greek words translated to the English word "poor" in the New Testament. Knowing these words will help us to understand what Jesus was saying. The first Greek word is "penes," and whenever it is translated to the English word "poor" it always refers to a man who is working to provide a meager living. It refers to a lack of material possessions and provision. This is <u>not</u> the word that Jesus used in this teaching. He used a word translated from the Greek word "ptochos." This word speaks of one who is completely destitute and has absolutely nothing at all; one who has no ability to obtain anything by his own power. Jesus is differentiating between the visible world (material possessions), and the condition of our hearts and spirits before God such that we can receive the fullness of His provision to us.

The word "poor" is found also in the Old Testament, predominately in the Psalms and in the Book of Isaiah. This word is translated from Hebrew words which refer to a humble and helpless man who has placed his complete trust in the Lord.

Putting the Greek word "ptochos" and the Hebrew words together in order to derive a good definition of the word "poor" as Jesus used it, we see clearly that it has nothing to do with material possessions. Jesus was effectively saying, "Blessed is the man who realizes his own utter helplessness and puts his whole trust in God, because his is the Kingdom of God."

This is a very important principle, and a key in the sense of our receiving the provision of God. It's possible for us to become so interested in blessing ourselves, in fulfilling desires of our own hearts, that we pursue plans and ways that are not of God. It is possible to be so consumed by the desire for the product that <u>we</u> try to produce it. But Jesus is saying that we are very blessed when our plans <u>don't</u> work if they are not in harmony with the will of God. Only complete trust in God will produce the results of the total provision of His kingdom. How do we draw upon that which He has promised? We must trust Him implicitly and completely.

Trust in the Lord

Proverbs 3:5-6 begins with the words, "Trust in the Lord with all thine heart." If our heart has nothing but the trust of God in it, then it is destitute of anything else. God is referring to our abandonment of all other alternatives. When people experience difficulties in life, some may say that God isn't fair, or God isn't good, or God isn't what He said He was going to be. However, the problem is not with God, it's with people! We get ourselves in trouble by keeping a "Plan B" alternative in the back of our mind. We formulate our own contingency or emergency plans. Sometimes we use the phrase "I must use wisdom" as an excuse for not trusting completely in God, and we sound very "spiritual" in saying that, but we are not fooling anyone, including ourselves.

God is not free to fully function in our life until we remove our hands from the "steering wheel" and submit ourselves wholly to Him. Until we give Him complete control, we are disqualifying ourselves from some of His blessings because we are not truly "poor in spirit." Very talented, intelligent, or gifted people sometimes have difficulty coming into the fullness of God in their lives because they can be more susceptible to pride, self-sufficiency, arrogance, and/or independence. They may think, "If God doesn't come through I'll just take care of it myself." That type of thinking reflects a heart full of alternatives, not a destitute heart. "Poor in spirit" means destitute and emptied of everything except trust in God. We are in the most advantageous position when we have no alternative but to trust in God.

No "Plan B"

When the Holy Spirit is working in our lives to make us "poor in spirit," there will likely be occasions when our self-formulated "Plan B" fails to succeed. Rather than become angry with God, we should thank the Holy Spirit for reminding us that we shouldn't have been "leaning" (Proverbs 3:5-6) on that plan. God will not allow some of our self-made plans to succeed because He wants the fullness of the Kingdom of God to be ours. Plan B can never deliver to us what the Kingdom of God will deliver to us. In order to be wholly yielded to the principles of the kingdom, we must empty ourselves (by the power of the Holy Spirit) of any and all alternatives which conflict with the principles of the kingdom. In our hearts, we don't want such conflict, because we love God and want to serve Him, but we still struggle with our selfish desires. Jesus understands that, and He also knows that many of His disciples go through struggles of their own making. We are fallible humans, and no matter how much we love the Lord, we can disobey him, become selfish, or hold back parts of our heart from Him.

We can possibly "get away with it" for a while, but sooner or later, God in His mercy will step in and "blow the whistle" on us, and we must face the music. It is not pleasant to our flesh when He does that, but it doesn't mean that He is angry at us. Why then does He do it? He does it because he doesn't want us to miss His best! He knows when we are going down a path that will not lead to the best of His blessings for us, even if we don't realize it ourselves. God is so committed to our success and our blessing that He has assigned the Holy Spirit to root out the things that continually keep us from His best in our lives. We must learn to be destitute, to be poor in spirit.

"Trust in the Lord with all thine heart and lean not unto thine own understanding." Many times our understanding will be contradictory to the will of the Lord. "In all thy ways acknowledge him and he shall direct thy paths." I have seen people with the attitude, "I'm angry with God. I've been in Sunday school since I was six years old. How did I get in such a mess? How could He have let me down?" The issue isn't whether they have been in Sunday school. The issue is: are they acknowledging the Lord in all their ways? It is the emptying of ourselves of every other alternative that brings the ultimate blessing and provision of God.

Making a U-Turn

When Jesus began His earthly ministry, He immediately introduced the message of the Kingdom of God. The first thing He said was, "Repent for the kingdom of heaven is at hand." The word "repent" means to turn and go the other way; to turn around one hundred eighty degrees. We often call that a "U-Turn." Jesus effectively said, "You've been wrong in your talking, thinking, and walking. You're so totally wrong that you must stop what you're doing, make a U-Turn, and let Me give you new direction in your life."

I find it interesting that Jesus' message to the Laodicean church in Revelation 3:17 was, "You say that you are *rich and increased with goods, and have need of nothing.* But I say you are *wretched, and miserable, and poor, and blind, and naked.*" He is effectively saying that many Christians have the attitude which conveys, "God is some kind of an addition to my life, some kind of an added blessing. He's kind of like the icing on my cake, or a little badge or button I wear." It cannot be that way! The only way to know the fullness of the blessings of the Kingdom of God is to submit completely to God. Total surrender. Total commitment. No compromise. We must make a decision to walk with the Lord, say what His Word says, and do what His Word instructs, without compromise. Our spirit must be void of anything but His way, emptied of every other alternative…poor in spirit. That's what Jesus was talking about! The Holy Spirit will continue to work in us until He roots out every alternative. We have things that we have come to believe are worth pursuing or leaning on, but He is so committed to bringing the blessing of God to us that He will not allow anything that will prevent it.

Make a Bigger Commitment

Jesus said, "No man can serve two masters; for either he will hate the one, and love the other; or else he will hold to the one, and despise the other." (Matthew 6:24) If you want more of the blessing of God, give yourself wholly to God. We must make a bigger commitment to Him, a determined decision that we will not hold anything back. We must pray, "Everything I have belongs to You, Lord. You are the focus of my life and my deepest desire. I choose to trust You wholly and completely. I abandon every other alternative. I have no faith in anything of this world's system or of my own making. Lord, You are my all. I'm destitute, and I empty myself before You that I might be filled with your provision."

That is what Jesus was teaching. He was effectively saying, "Do you want to be a disciple? Come close to Me. I want to tell you one of the secrets...You must be poor in spirit." When we make a deeper commitment, we must understand that when the Holy Spirit begins to work in our lives, we may feel like we are losing everything we've ever had. I have heard people say, "Things didn't start going wrong until I became a Christian." If that is your experience, I encourage you to hold on, because you haven't seen the good yet. God has provision beyond anything you could ever attain on your own. What has happened is that the things that seemed to be your strengths in the past have become totally ineffective now. They are old tools that don't work any longer.

For example, how many of us once thought that we were very wise, only to learn that our wisdom was in fact flawed, and we were often wrong? We must forsake our wisdom and seek God's wisdom. He declared in James 5:1, "If any of you lack wisdom, let him ask of God, that giveth to all men liberally, and upbraideth not; and it shall be given him." The real answer is to turn away from every alternative in favor of totally pursuing God and His ways. We are favored, blessed, when we reach that place of being poor in spirit, for only then do we become candidates to receive the fullness of the Lord in our lives.

A Challenge to Surrender!

If you desire victory over things that have been troubling you for a long time in your life, I challenge you to abandon every other alternative and seek the Lord with all of your heart. I have found that the greatest place of victory lies in total and unconditional surrender to Jesus Christ. "Nothing in my hand I bring only to thy cross I cling." Jesus is everything to me. When I compare Him to anything in which I have prided myself, I must admit, like the apostle Paul, that it is all dung (garbage). Paul listed his pedigree and all of his "credentials" in Philippians 3:5, "Circumcised the eighth day, of the stock of Israel, of the tribe of Benjamin, an Hebrew of the Hebrews; as touching the law, a Pharisee." Paul had credentials that were far more impressive than most of us, yet he declared that they all added up to nothing...they were all refuse. Why? Because Paul had become poor in spirit. He was essentially saying, "I throw them all away, I empty my heart, I become poor in spirit that I may win Christ. I lean not on the strength of these accomplishments or credentials, but instead I give myself wholly to the Lord."

Paul said it well in Romans 12:1-2, "I beseech you therefore, brethren, by the mercies of God, that ye present your bodies a living sacrifice, holy, acceptable unto God, which is your reasonable service. And be not conformed to this world; but be ye transformed by the renewing of your mind, that ye may prove what is that good, and acceptable, and perfect, will of God." God will bring you to the place that you realize the only one you can really depend upon is Him. The only answers that will always be right are *His*. The only direction that never leads you down a dead end is *His*. The only strength that will never fail is *His*. The only peace that will stand in every storm is *His*. The only joy that is unspeakable and full of glory is *His*. The only hope that never disappoints is *His*. The only love that is indescribable, unending, and unfailing is *His*....and when He brings you to that place called "poor in spirit," the provisions of the Kingdom of God are *yours*. Blessed are the poor in spirit!

Chapter 3

Blessed Are They That Mourn

The second of eight principles we find in the Beatitudes is, "Blessed are they that mourn; for they shall be comforted." This is a saying that has often been misunderstood or misinterpreted based on the meaning of two key words - "mourn" and "comforted."

As we study this principle based on the condition/provision structure that we discussed in Chapter 1, we see that the *condition* is to "mourn," and the *provision* is to "be comforted."

The Provision: ...Shall Be Comforted

What does it mean to be comforted? The Greek word from which "comforted" is translated is *parakleo*. It means "called near; called close; strengthened, refreshed, fulfilled." The word *parakleo* is very much like the Greek word *parakletos*, which is the word Jesus used to describe the Holy Spirit as the "Comforter." The Spirit is the one that "comes alongside us," the one that is near us, the one that makes the presence of Jesus real to us, and the one that strengthens and fulfills us. In this Beatitude, Jesus was making an exciting promise that the ministry of the Holy Spirit will be made available to us. We "shall be comforted." The mission of the Holy Spirit will be experienced in our lives. The Holy Spirit will not simply be a doctrinal concept to us. Rather, His person, mission, and manifestation will be very real to us. God's plan and provision is for every believer to walk in the Spirit, in the comfort of God.

This was declared prophetically in Isaiah 61:1-3, which Jesus quoted in the synagogue at Nazareth at the very beginning of His earthly ministry (Luke 4:18-19). The first phrase of Isaiah 61:1 states, "The Spirit of the Lord God is upon me." Similarly, Acts 10:38 declares that God "anointed Jesus of Nazareth." Because the Holy Spirit was upon Jesus, His mission was (and still is, through His people) to "preach good tidings to the meek, bind up the brokenhearted, proclaim liberty to the captives, and the opening of the prison to them that are bound. To proclaim the acceptable year of the Lord, and the day of vengeance of our God; *to comfort all that mourn*; To appoint unto them that mourn in Zion, to give unto them beauty for ashes, the oil of joy for mourning, the garment of praise for the spirit of heaviness; that they might be called trees of righteousness, the planting of the Lord, that he might be glorified." (Isaiah 61:1-3)

"The Spirit of the Lord is upon me." The words that follow that introductory statement define the mission of the Spirit of the Lord. The mission has not changed; only the mechanism. Rather than the mission being manifested through the physical body of Jesus, as it was during His earthly ministry, it is now being manifested through the spiritual Body of Christ (the universal body of believers). One of the important aspects of the mission and ministry of the Holy Spirit is to comfort people. That is an exciting provision and something I believe we all desire and need. What is the *condition* for us to receive this wonderful *provision*?

The Condition: They That Mourn...

The *condition* is to be in a state of *mourning*. Jesus said that we are highly favored when we experience the condition of mourning, but what did He mean by "mourning?" If we interpret the word "mourn" as it is commonly used, we may conclude it means "blessed is the man that cries, wails, moans, groans, complains, and pouts, because he's going to get his own way and be appeased." However, that isn't what "mourn" means at all in Matthew 5:4.

The word "mourn" is translated from the Greek word *pentheo*, which means "a deep inner spirit burden." It has nothing to do with the number of tears rolling down our cheeks or how loudly we cry, but rather with what the Holy Spirit does in our hearts. *Pentheo* is the strongest Greek word of many which are translated "mourn," and it speaks of a condition that refers to the deepest, darkest, most impossible situation that the mind of man can conceive.

Worldly Sorrow vs. Godly Sorrow

We will examine the condition of mourning in two dimensions: first as it applies to us personally and secondly as we mourn for the sake of others. A phrase that is used in Scripture is "Godly sorrow." We must understand that there is a "worldly sorrow" which is different from a "Godly sorrow." Worldly sorrow is when someone is mournful because they were caught, or because they are experiencing the consequences of their actions. However, Godly sorrow is quite different. The Bible declares that "Godly sorrow worketh repentance" (II Corinthians 7:10), and to *repent* means to turn from the wrong way to another way. It is not sufficient to have worldly sorrow when we are dealing with sin. Worldly sorrow can cause us to shed tears yet never change our lifestyle. However, the Holy Spirit will continue to work in us until we change our lifestyle, because repentance is to be a way of life.

The Apostle Paul wrote in II Corinthians 7:9-10, "Now I rejoice, not that ye were made sorry, but that ye sorrowed to repentance: for ye were made sorry after a Godly manner, that ye might receive damage by us in nothing. For Godly sorrow worketh repentance to salvation not to be repented of: but the sorrow of the world worketh death." He was effectively saying, "I do not rejoice simply because you're sorry. I rejoice that your sorrow brought repentance because the result will be a redirection of your lifestyle 'to salvation.'" He was speaking of more than being born again; he was referring to wholeness of spirit, soul, and body which is "not to be repented of." That means "not to be revoked." It is irrevocable! Worldly sorrow only results in death, because unless we change our direction and our ways, we can be sorry repeatedly, yet we are still headed toward death. It does no good to shed a few tears along the road to death. We need more than sorrow for what we've done - we need to turn from death to life. That's what Godly sorrow produces.

Every one of us who is a born-again believer has

experienced a turning from death to life. There was a moment in each of our lives when the Holy Spirit came to us in the inner recesses of our being. It was more than intellectual knowledge, more than emotion, more than a preacher encouraging us to make a decision for God. When God gets hold of a person's heart and convinces him that he is a sinner, the result is a turning around, a change, a different lifestyle. It is called "repentance."

Repentance

Repentance is an attitude and a lifestyle. When we begin to drift away from a repentant lifestyle, wander from the "narrow road," and start following old sinful ways, the Holy Spirit will begin to work on our hearts. Did you ever try shedding a few tears and going to sleep when you haven't repented? Or perhaps call someone and ask them to pray for you when you haven't repented? It's very uncomfortable and nearly impossible. If the Holy Spirit is working on us, when we don't repent we feel miserable, because He is calling for a change of lifestyle. People that think they can "act holy" in church, going through all the "religious" motions, then go out and live in sin are missing the mark badly. People in that condition will find no true "comfort" in their lives. They may think, "Why isn't the Holy Spirit working in my life? Where is the anointing, the peace, and the power in my life? Why doesn't God use me in a greater way?"

This is the reality: the Holy Spirit cannot fully work in our lives until we have Godly sorrow and repentance. When Jesus says, "Blessed are they that mourn," He is speaking of Godly sorrow. When the Holy Spirit begins to work deeply in our hearts, He brings true conviction. It is not simply "feeling badly" about something. It is a deep anguish of the spirit. The cry of our hearts should be, "Oh Lord, I want to be free, holy, and just." When we travail and sorrow and truly repent, Jesus says that we are blessed and highly favored of God. We are blessed when He won't let us drift off to sleep until we repent. He "meddles" deeply in our hearts because if He didn't, we would be heading toward spiritual death. When He "digs deeply" into our hearts, it may be uncomfortable and we may not like it at the time, but He truly is favoring us because He loves us too much to leave us in our sins and struggles.

A Burden for Others

Having Godly sorrow for our own sins is only one dimension of mourning, because we don't live unto ourselves, but also for others. Cain asked a question that we all confront at some point in our lives, "Am I my brother's keeper?" (Genesis 4:9) Can any of us find a path through life where what happens to other people doesn't matter nor affect us? Not if we are a child of God! When we pray, "God use me," we may have in mind a far-reaching, highly visible ministry, but sometimes what God has in mind is waking us up at three o'clock in the morning with a burden to pray for someone else. That is being used by God as much as preaching to ten thousand people. Romans 8:26 declares, "Likewise the Spirit helpeth our infirmities; for we know not what we should pray for as we ought." In and of ourselves, we do not know for *what* to pray, or for *whom* to pray, or even *how* to pray. "But the Spirit itself maketh intercession for us with groanings which cannot be uttered." The word uttered means "cannot be expressed in words," and refers to times when words are inadequate. There are times when we can't frame a thought within the context of our vocabulary, but deep within our heart and spirit there is a burden and a deep compassion and cry for others.

For example, there may be someone that the Holy Spirit lays on our heart, and a deep cry of prayer rises from within. I am referring to a cry that goes beyond the thoughts of our mind and the words of our vocabulary. It goes beyond something that we are contriving within our mind. What is the result? The Holy Spirit begins moving to accomplish His purpose. We may be binding the forces of the enemy, warring in the spirit. We may be pleading the cause of another. It releases the ministry of the Holy Spirit. "They shall be comforted." The Holy Spirit will give "Beauty for ashes, the oil of joy for mourning, the garment of praise for the spirit of heaviness." When a deep cry and burden arises from our hearts and the Holy Spirit is released to produce change, God works through His people to produce results.

The Holy Spirit is going to use us to affect the lives of others. We will come to know the walk of mourning. We will come to know the cry of the spirit for the wounded, the hurting, and those that are lukewarm and without a hunger for God. If we really want the favor of God on our lives, we must make ourselves available to mourn for others.

Sowing in Tears

Psalm 126:1-6 declares, "When the Lord turned again the captivity of Zion, we were like them that dream. Then was our mouth filled with laughter, and our tongue with singing; then said they among the heathen, The Lord hath done great things for us; whereof we are glad. Turn again our captivity, O Lord, as the streams in the south. They that sow in tears shall reap in joy. He that goeth forth and weepeth, bearing precious seed, shall doubtless come again with rejoicing, bringing his sheaves with him."

Please note that Psalm 126 does not say "they that shed tears," but rather "they that sow in tears." *There is an important difference between shedding tears and sowing in tears.* Shedding tears is simply an emotional action or reaction. We may shed tears because of an emotional pressure, an emotional high, or an emotional low. I'm not against shedding tears, but it is not the same as sowing in tears. When we sow in tears, we are planting something. We are setting something in motion that will bring forth fruit. We are not simply releasing an emotion; we are setting something into action. He that sows tears is weeping, "bearing precious seed." Psalm 56:8-9 declares, "Thou tellest my wanderings: put thou my tears into thy bottle; are they not in thy book? When I cry unto thee, then shall mine enemies turn back; this I know; for God is for me." The Psalmist is referring to a Godly sorrow, a work of the Spirit, and He says that when that happens, our enemies will turn back because God is with us when we sow in tears.

There are three instances in Scripture in which I believe

Jesus sowed in tears and mourned in the Spirit. By examining these three instances, we can better understand how the Spirit works inside us to produce the condition of mourning.

A Burden for Those Close to Us

When Jesus stood at the grave of Lazarus, He wept. (John 11:35) Many of the people who were there that day thought He was weeping because His friend Lazarus had died. However, He was really weeping because of their unbelief. He wasn't weeping at the power of death. He was weeping at sin, because unbelief is sin. Why did Jesus weep at sin? Because the people there that day had concluded that death was more powerful than life even though Jesus, the giver of life eternal and abundant, was standing there! He stood there in front of the grave to demonstrate to them that life was greater than death! Jesus didn't weep at death; He wept at sin. The weeping was the Holy Spirit working within His spirit. His heart was broken. As He wept at their unbelief, He released the work of the Holy Spirit that brought life and they were ultimately comforted as Lazarus was raised from the dead.

A Burden for Those to Whom We Are Sent

The second place in Scripture which refers to Jesus weeping is found in Matthew Chapter 23. His ministry was drawing to a close and He was overlooking Jerusalem. He was looking in the Spirit at a people for whom He had come and for whom He would soon be dying on a cross. He lamented that if they would only have trusted in Him, truly heard what He said, and followed what He taught, they would be free. See Him as He groans from His spirit. Hear His deep burden and the cry of the Father's heart. Jesus cried, "O Jerusalem, Jerusalem, thou that killest the prophets, and stonest them which are sent unto thee, how often would I have gathered thy children together, even as a hen gathereth her chickens under her wings, and ye would not!" (Matthew 23:37)   What was He weeping about? Sin!   Rejecting Jesus is the ultimate sin.   Yes, morality, goodness, and similar things are important, but the bottom line is whether a person has received Jesus or not.   People can live very good moral lives, but if Jesus isn't living within them, they are spiritually dead.

A Burden for the World

There is one more instance of Jesus' sorrow, and it occurred in the Garden of Gethsemane.   If we combine the account from Luke Chapter 22 with a companion verse from Hebrews Chapter 4, we find that in the garden, a few short hours before Calvary, Jesus sweat "as it were great drops of blood," (Luke 22:44) and His heart was broken for the world - He was "touched with the feeling of our infirmities." (Hebrews 4:15)

Three Burdens

In summary, I believe that Scripture shows us that Jesus wept first for those that were near Him (at Lazarus' grave), secondly for those to whom He was sent (the city of Jerusalem), and thirdly for the world.   I believe that the work of the Holy

Spirit will touch us such that we will have three similar burdens. First, He'll give us a burden for those that are near us - for our unsaved loved ones and friends. Secondly, He'll give us a burden for those to whom He sends us, perhaps our neighborhood, workplace, class, or fellowship group. Thirdly, the Holy Spirit will burden us for the world because His burden is for the world. We know the Holy Spirit is truly working in us when we begin to be burdened for people we don't even know. The Holy Spirit may give us burdens for people that others have given up on because He hasn't given up on them!

We are blessed and favored by the Lord when we experience genuine Godly sorrow for ourselves and/or for others. If we embrace it and allow the Holy Spirit to intercede through us, the ministry of the Spirit will produce results in that person or situation. In fact, entire nations can be turned to God when the Holy Spirit puts Godly sorrow in the hearts of the people of God and they respond in obedient and heartfelt prayer. (II Chronicles 7:14) Prayer isn't academic or insignificant. Prayer is God "tampering" with our lives so that He might comfort and minister His life to those in need.

I encourage you as a believer that when you experience Godly sorrow, God is favoring you. Don't treat it lightly, dismiss it, ignore it, reject it, be embarrassed by it, or apologize for it. Thank the Lord for it. He's favored you because life will come out of it. Blessed are they that mourn!

Chapter 4

Blessed Are the Meek

The third of the eight principles of blessing as taught by Jesus in the Beatitudes is "Blessed are the meek for they shall inherit the earth." We will first examine the *provision* (inheriting the earth), and then the *condition* (being meek).

The Provision: ...Shall Inherit the Earth

What does it mean to "inherit the earth?" First, we must take note of the word "inherit." Jesus did not use any of the verbs "earn," "purchase" or "conquer." He used the verb *inherit* which means "to receive a gift from a predecessor." Further, what does He mean by inheriting the *earth*? Jesus was not speaking of geography or real estate. We can be so carnally minded that we interpret things in a natural sense, but I believe that Scripture helps us to understand Jesus' spiritual message, as Psalm 2:8 declares, "Ask of me and I shall <u>*give*</u> thee the heathen for thine <u>*inheritance*</u>, and the uttermost parts of the earth for thy possession."

Jesus was speaking about eternal things, about earth's occupants, its <u>people</u>, <u>not</u> about land. The Bible declares that "the earth is the Lord's and the fullness thereof" (Psalm 24:1) and God "owns the cattle on a thousand hills" (Psalm 50:10)...and we know that He also owns the hills themselves as well! Jesus was referring to <u>people</u> when He referred to the inheritance that He wants to give to us as believers. *<u>Jesus didn't die to purchase property, He died to redeem people</u>*. We should be excited when we think about winning the world for Jesus Christ. The angels in heaven rejoice when even <u>one</u> sinner repents (Luke 15:7, 10), and Jesus has promised us the <u>world</u>!

We can't buy or earn an inheritance. We can only receive it. "Ask of me and I will <u>give</u> thee…" (Psalm 2:8) When a group of believers dares to stand up and trust God for the uttermost parts of the earth and for the heathen, He will joyfully grant it. We don't need to travel thousands of miles to find people that need God - they are all around us every day.

The Condition: The Meek...

Because "inheriting the earth" is such an incredible *provision*, the *condition* must be very important. If we have the desire to inherit the earth, it is because that desire was placed in our hearts by God. Why do we awaken in the middle of the night and cry for lost souls? Why do we joyfully give a tithe to the work of the Lord? Why are we moved to do as Paul wrote in Romans 12:1, "Present your bodies a living sacrifice, holy, acceptable unto God, which is your reasonable service?" Why? *<u>Because the value that Jesus places on people has been placed in our hearts</u>*. God paid the price for people, and He wants to deliver them. He wants "all men" (and women and children) to be saved. (I Timothy 2:4) What is the Holy Spirit doing in us, the people of God, such that we can continue to experience inheriting the earth, the heathen for our possession, in an ever increasing way? According to Jesus, the Holy Spirit will make us meek...but what does it mean to be meek?

When most of us think of the word "meek," we have something in our minds which is entirely different than what Jesus meant by the word. The word "meek" is translated from the Greek word *praos,* which is one of the most powerful words in the entire Greek language. First, we must realize that *meek does not mean weak*. It does not refer to cowardice, spinelessness, or ineffectiveness. The word *praos* refers to one who is under divine control and whose will is wholly surrendered to the will of God. We all know that there are times when our biggest enemy is not the devil, but rather our own self-will, which can sometimes be contrary to the will of God. Man's will, submitted to the will of God and brought into harmony with the will and purposes of God, results in the manifestation of the will of God.

Relying on the Holy Spirit

Since the will of God is that we ask Him to "give us the heathen for our inheritance, and the uttermost parts of the earth for our possession," we can be certain He will bring that provision as we come into harmony with His will. However, even though we may possess that desire, we will only see the manifestation (*provision*), when we identify with the *condition* (meekness). It is very sad when we spend days, months, years, or even a lifetime, struggling to accomplish what only He can accomplish, attempting to produce what only He can produce. There is a Godly desire in our hearts, but sometimes in our own attempt to bring to pass the purposes of God, we overlook the fact that the Holy Spirit has been divinely commissioned by the Father to do His work in the earth. Jesus has been appointed the Lord of the Harvest (Matthew 9:38), and we are simply instruments to carry out His mission. We do not know all of the strategies or the master plan, but we are very privileged to be involved with the one (Jesus) who is in charge. We don't see the "big picture" nor understand how to accomplish the goal, but He does!

Sometimes when we do something that seems to produce great results for the kingdom of God, we tend to treat it as some kind of "formula" that we could repeat over and over and see similar results. However, neither our formula nor our labor brings results. It is only the presence of Jesus and the work of the Spirit that produces results! Unless the Holy Spirit is at work, we can never produce results. We can preach the Word, but not even one soul will be saved unless the Holy Spirit is actively involved. We can do nothing without Him. Our Bible knowledge, communication skills, eloquence, and charisma are all woefully inadequate and ineffective without the touch of the Holy Spirit. The Spirit, not us, is the one that convinces and convicts people. Sometimes Christians get frustrated when they sense that they are not as effective as they once were in leading people to the Lord. They may feel that they are backsliding, but perhaps it is because they are relying on their own knowledge, techniques, or experience, instead of relying on the Holy Spirit as they once did. In a sense, they have become less meek over time and thus are not receiving the inheritance they once did.

The Lesson of the Brahma Bull

I read a story some time ago that illustrates this truth beautifully. A farmer in a remote area of Kenya found that using modern transportation such as a truck to move goods from one point to another was ineffective because the roads were so poor. Likewise, the nature of the terrain and the soil rendered the use of a tractor ineffective for farming. So he turned to raising Brahma bulls. These bulls are as mean as they look, but when properly trained, they are very valuable and effective in hauling heavy loads from one point to another, pulling plows, and preparing the ground for seeding. Because the bulls are so valuable, they come at a very high price. Raising Brahma bulls is an honored occupation in that area.

The farmer related the difficulty of training a Brahma bull to the point at which it could be used effectively for the work which must be done. The bull had all of the raw attributes that were needed. The bull possessed the strength, endurance, and ability to endure long, hot days and conditions which even horses could not endure. But the Brahma bull had one big problem - a stubborn self-will that was almost unreal.

Brahma bulls are born with that stubborn nature and their constitution seems to communicate, "No one will harness me!" The farmer had the difficult task of breaking the will of the bull to the point that all of the bull's attributes and energy could be harnessed to produce useful results. Unharnessed and uncontrolled energy is useless and even destructive in some cases. The farmer would take a bull and tie him to a yoke. The bull would then paw, bellow, twist, turn, kick, and fight. This would go on for a period of time, but with proper patience and commitment on the part of the farmer, the self-will of the Brahma bull would eventually be broken.

It is important to understand that the bull itself wasn't broken - simply its will to "do its own thing." The bull didn't realize that all of the energy and strength it possessed was very useful if it was tied to a plow or a trailer. However, if the owner allowed the bull to "do its own thing," the bull would live its whole life essentially wasting its immense strength and energy, never accomplishing the good for which it was meant.

We must admit that, like the bull, we all have a natural tendency to stubbornly live our own lives and "do our own thing in our own way." However, if we continue this pattern of behavior, we could spend years, or even a lifetime, accomplishing little or nothing of eternal consequence. We can do much pawing, snorting, and arm waving. We can kick up massive amounts of dust, yet never carry a load from point A to point B, and never plow any ground. I have spoken to brokenhearted people with tears rolling down their cheeks, pouring out their hearts and effectively saying, "I've done a lot of bellowing and raised a lot of dust, and I don't have anything to show for it." Perhaps there is nothing quite as tragic as a life wasted.

The Meekness of Moses

The Holy Spirit will come to us and affirm that God has placed in us positive attributes, useful energy, talents, anointing, and abilities that can produce eternal results for the Kingdom of

God. He has given us "tools" that can be used to reach the unsaved and touch the four corners of the earth. We have more giftings in us than we will ever realize until we are harnessed.

One of the reasons we quarrel with each other so much is that we are unharnessed. Numbers 12:3 declares that Moses was meeker than any man on the face of the earth. We know from Scripture that Moses was not spineless. He was a man of great courage and character, a man of action, but he could have never accomplished all that God called him to do if he hadn't been submitted to God and became God-directed. He was a strong man, but he was under God's control, in God's harness, and he was meek. There were a number of occasions in which he went to God and humbly asked, "What do we do now?"

An excellent illustration of Moses' submission of his self-will to God occurred when his sister Marian and brother Aaron rebelled against him. The Bible says they rebelled because he had married an Ethiopian woman. They effectively said, "Do you think you're the only one that hears from God, Moses?" If we read that story carefully, we observe that Moses did not defend himself nor fight back, and in the end God vindicated Moses. (Numbers 12:1-16)

Meekness is about "controlled strength." Sometimes it takes more strength <u>not</u> to fight than it does to fight. Sometimes, it takes more strength <u>not</u> to defend ourselves than it does to defend ourselves. Most of us have experienced being falsely accused. If we are unharnessed, our natural reaction is to do all in our power to vindicate ourselves. We expend valuable energy trying to vindicate ourselves or make ourselves look good in the eyes of others. Imagine what kind of power we would have in the Body of Christ if we would each be expending our energy toward winning souls rather than quarrelling among ourselves! Imagine what could happen if we all had our arms around one another whether we interpreted every Scripture verse the same way or not. Can you imagine the power of our combined *controlled strength*?

Jesus, the Ultimate Example of Controlled Strength

It is very important to understand that we must become God-controlled, harnessed with God. For example, II Corinthians 6:2 states, "We then as workers together *with* God..." (as opposed to working *for* God). How do we bring our self-will under His direction? Jesus was speaking to believers in Matthew 11:28 when He said, "Come unto me, all ye that labour and are heavy-laden, and I will give you rest. Take my yoke upon you and learn of me, for I am *meek*." What was the secret to the power in the earthly ministry of Jesus? He was meek, harnessed to the will of the Father. *Jesus is the ultimate example of controlled strength*. Jesus said, "I only do the things which I see the Father do." (John 5:19)

One of the first things Satan tried to do to Jesus on the mountain (Luke Chapter 4) was to tempt Him to demonstrate His power, to release His energy inconsistent with the will of the Father. Satan tempted him by effectively saying, "Show me! Are you really the Son of God? Go ahead, jump off this mountain. It's written in Scripture that He will give His angels charge over you. Show me!" Jesus effectively responded, "I'm not going to divert the energy that My Father has given Me." Satan continued to tempt Him, "Command these stones that they be made bread." If we were in Jesus' sandals that day, we may have been tempted to respond to that kind of a challenge by saying, "I am going to show you! I'll not only make these stones bread. I'll shove that bread down your throat!" Praise God that Jesus is meek, and that He truly exhibited controlled strength.

Perhaps the ultimate challenge came when the people looked at Jesus as He was hanging on the cross and said, "If thou be the Son of God, come down from the cross." (Mark 15:30) Make no mistake about it, Jesus could have answered that challenge by coming down from the cross. However, He was meek, and because the will of the Father was that the sacrifice be made, Jesus remained on the cross. The strongest man that ever lived chose to willingly lay down his life in the presence of weaklings who were tempting Him and mocking Him. Talk about controlled strength!

Rest in God

Every blessing we enjoy today is a result of the fact that Jesus knelt in the Garden of Gethsemane and won the battle over self-will. He pronounced, "Nevertheless not my will but thine be done." (Luke 22:42) Speaking of Jesus, I Peter 2:23 declares, "Who, when he was reviled, reviled not again; when he suffered, he threatened not; but committed himself to him that judgeth righteously." Jesus committed Himself to His Father, the one that judges righteously. This is exactly what we must do.

Hebrews 4:9 states, "There remaineth therefore a rest to the people of God." What is the "rest" for the people of God? It is the confidence in knowing that when I have submitted myself to Him and His will, He is committed to take care of me, guide me, and lead me. It is the knowledge that He is on my side and I am going to win.

There is a peace, a rest, in God. In each of our lives, we only see portions of what God has put inside us. Only God knows the deposit He put in us when we were born, which I believe He ordained long before birth. The cry of my heart is that whatever God has seen fit to put in me when He ordained my birth, I want all of it - every bit of it - all of the energy, the potential, and every attribute submitted to the Lord. I want to be yoked with Him to the point that my life will result in accomplishing the will of the Father. Often, I don't even know what the will of the Father is in a specific sense, but I know in a general sense. I don't know exactly what God is going to have me do for the rest of my life. I have an idea what I've been doing the first seven and a half decades, but I don't know for certain what is in my future. Regardless of what we've done, and what we know or do not know, we can come into rest when we are yoked with Jesus.

Put On Meekness

Paul wrote to the believers at Colossae, "Put on therefore, as the elect of God, holy and beloved, bowels of mercies, kindness, humbleness of mind, meekness, longsuffering." (Colossians 3:12) Putting on *meekness* is an action that we take, something to which we submit, a decision we make, saying, "I am going to surrender my will to the will of God." Proverbs 16:32 declares, "He that is slow to anger is better than the mighty; and he that ruleth his spirit than he that taketh a city." To "rule our spirit" means to come under the control of, and be subjected to, the will of the Father.

Jesus is saying that the Holy Spirit is at work in our lives because He wants to produce something powerful through us. We must embrace and believe the promise of "the heathen for our inheritance and the uttermost parts of the earth for our possession" (Psalm 2:8), which results from meeting the condition of surrendering our will to the Lord's will. Jesus trusted the Holy Spirit, and we must do the same.

Saul's Story

Saul of Tarsus, who would later become known as the Apostle Paul, had many things "under control." He thought he knew "the will of God" for him - to persecute and kill Christians. He possessed deep knowledge of the Scriptures, having been trained by one of the most prominent Rabbis of his day. Saul may have been one of the most intelligent, learned men that ever lived. He had impeccable credentials. Yet, he was misusing his God-given energy by doing things such as holding the coats of the people that were stoning Stephen. (Acts 7:58) Saul's self-will was badly out of step with the will of God, yet he didn't know it. He seemingly had the whole world at his fingertips, and he was very religious.

However, Acts Chapter 9 gives the account of how the

Lord of the Harvest reached out and knocked Saul to the ground. Suddenly, he was lying in the dust. We have several alternatives when we have been reduced to dust. One alternative is to become angry and complain because we are dirty, and cry out to God, "You have ruined my plans and my life!" Saul chose another alternative. Saul called Him "Lord," which was a sign of reverence and submission, and a very significant word for Saul to use.

Jesus said, "Saul, you have struggled, kicking against the goads." A goad was a sharpened stick that was used to prod oxen. Saul hadn't realized that he was kicking against the goads. In fact, he thought he was doing well and even pleasing God! However, Jesus effectively was saying, "Saul, I love you so much that I'm not going to allow you to continue down the wrong trail and continue doing what you have been doing. If you do, you will ruin and waste your life. I didn't knock you down to make you dirty. I knocked you down so that you would look up and listen to Me, repent, and set your life on the right path. When I lift you up, we are going to do things that the world will never forget. Centuries from now, people will read the books you will write as you are inspired by the Spirit of God. Your life will affect many lives for eternity!" Saul humbly and meekly responded, "What wilt thou have me to do?" He was effectively saying, "Jesus, it is Your will that matters most from now on." Saul had become one of the meek. He was not weak. He was never weak. He simply redirected his tremendous energy in God's direction rather than his own, and he would become known as the Apostle Paul, a glorious example of controlled strength!

Harnessed Energy

When water flows over a waterfall, there is only the sound of the falling water on the rocks. However, if that falling water is harnessed and used to turn a generator, useful electricity is produced. As lighting flashes through the sky, there is brilliant light, but if its electrical potential is tapped, incredible power can result from that harnessed energy. The energy in which Jesus is interested is neither waterfalls nor lightning. The energy in which He is interested is what He has put inside each of us. I don't know all the answers concerning my life or anyone else's, but one thing I know is that we cannot miss when we slip our neck into the yoke with Jesus.

Our success in life has nothing to do with our charisma, beauty, ability, or intelligence. It has everything to do with being yoked with Jesus. He invited each of us, "Come unto me, all ye that labor and are heavy laden." Perhaps you are tired, weary, and even exhausted with life. Even if you are trying to live a good Christian life, you can become yoked with religion, tradition, doctrine, or self serving, and become weary and frustrated. You need to be yoked with Jesus. Blessed are the meek!

Chapter 5

Blessed Are They Which Do Hunger and Thirst After Righteousness

Matthew 5:6 declares, "Blessed are they which do hunger and thirst after righteousness for they shall be filled." We are highly favored of God when the Holy Spirit produces hunger and thirst after righteousness - that is the *condition*. The result, the *provision*, is we shall be filled. Therefore, as the Holy Spirit works in each of our lives creating hunger and thirst after righteousness, we should identify it, embrace it, respond to it, rejoice in it, and know that we are about to come into a place of being fulfilled.

The Provision: Shall Be Filled

The Greek word *chortazo* is the word which is translated "filled" and it means "to be satisfied, to be complete, to be whole, or to be fulfilled." It is important that we understand this as "filled" as opposed to "empty." It has nothing to do with the quantity contained, but it has everything to do with a state of bliss, of being wholly satisfied. This is contentment such that our heart is at rest and in peace, and there is no void or emptiness in us. That is a tremendous promise given to us by God.

We can be filled with many things in the world and yet not be satisfied. Many people are filled with activities, events, and pursuits, but those things in and of themselves do not satisfy. True satisfaction can only be found in Christ Jesus. He's saying to those of us that will take the time to be alone with Him that He desires to satisfy us, and He tells us how He goes about doing it. Here is the condition: "I will cause you to hunger and thirst after righteousness."

Physical Hunger and Thirst

God designed a tremendous phenomenon in our physical hunger and thirst. Sometimes we take these things for granted. Hunger and thirst are so much a part of our natural lives that we may not realize the significance and importance of the mechanisms which God built into us. He knew, for instance, that in order for life to be sustained, we were going to have to receive nourishment.

Hunger is a physiological sensation. The appetite center in the human body is called the appestat. It is comprised of activity in both our stomach and our brain. When we experience hunger it not only comes from our stomach, but also from our brain. They work together.

In God's physiological design of the human body, He created the duodenum, located at the bottom part of the small intestine, which sends out a signal when the body needs food. The stomach reacts and the muscles begin to cramp as the need for food is sensed by the body. However, not only is there something going on in the stomach, but there is also something happening in the brain.

The hypothalamus of the brain is comprised of bilateral nerve cells. These nerve cells are designed such that on one side, the lateral nuclei react and produce a sensation, saying, "You need to eat." On the other side, the ventromedial nuclei produce just the opposite sensation and say, "Stop eating." It's awesome the way God designed us with this on/off mechanism in our brain.

With regard to thirst, God designed something called osmoreceptors which are sensitive to the balance between salt and water in our bodies. The osmoreceptors maintain the proper water level because if our water level gets too low we will experience dehydration. We must have sufficient enough water in order to function and live.

When the duodenum and hypothalamus signal to us, we must respond and receive nourishment. The body receives nourishment and life is sustained. God has built these devices into us so that we can enjoy health, strength, and the fullness of life. Indeed, we are "fearfully and wonderfully made." (Psalm 139:14)

God so beautifully designed our bodies, and we really only understand a little bit of it but He knew this was going to be necessary in order for life to be sustained. So what do we do? We learn how to respond to that. When the duodenum or hypothalamus starts working, we don't ignore them, or we would starve. We respond to that and we take nourishment. The body receives that and life is given. The osmoreceptors signal our need for liquids and we respond to that. We've learned that

God has built these devices into us so that we can enjoy health, strength, and the fullness of life.

Spiritual Hunger and Thirst

Jesus is teaching us about spiritual hunger and thirst by using the analogy of physical hunger and thirst. He is effectively saying that the Holy Spirit is charged with creating in us a spiritual hunger and thirst. The Greek word for hunger is *peinao*, and the Greek word for thirst is *dipsao*. Both of these Greek words carry the meaning of being desperate for nourishment, for food and water. They carry the idea of experiencing gnawing pains and literally starving to death or dying of thirst. They are two of the strongest words in the Greek language and they describe a condition that is a matter of life or death. It's not like casually saying, "It is noon so it's time to eat and drink something." Rather, it's like desperately saying, "If I don't eat something I'm going to die. I'm at the very brink of starvation. I am famished. If I don't drink something, I am literally going to die of thirst."

Most of us in America may use such phrases occasionally, but we likely don't truly understand them. Tragically though, many people around the world live daily at the brink of death due to starvation or lack of clean drinking water. When they eat or drink, it is literally a life saving action. It is not just a time consuming activity or habit. It is a matter of life and death. That's the meaning of the words translated "hunger" and "thirst" in the Greek language. It's neither trivial nor optional; it's essential. It <u>must</u> happen or we will not live.

When we experience desperate spiritual hunger and thirst, it is because the Holy Spirit is at work in us. Deep spiritual hunger and thirst do not produce simply a casual interest in God; they produce a deep *passion* for God. It's the difference between saying, "Please don't tell me I have to sing that chorus again" as opposed to saying, "Jesus, I can't sing enough about you because I love you so much." It's the difference between asking, "Do I have to read my Bible every day?" as opposed to saying, "Where is my Bible? I need the Word of God to make it through today." It's not simply a daily habitual activity; it's a matter of life. Jesus is saying that only the Holy Spirit can create this in us.

An Ongoing Condition, Not a One Time Experience

The very tense of these Greek verbs indicate that hunger and thirst are continuing actions. They aren't simply one time experiences, but rather something which will be intermittently intense throughout our entire lifetime. Likewise, the Holy Spirit will create a hunger and thirst in us such that we want more of God's presence and His Word. Jesus was literally saying, "Blessed is he that *continues* to hunger and thirst."

Righteousness: The Object of Hunger and Thirst

The object of our hunger and thirst is critically important. Some people have an ungodly appetite or thirst for ungodly things. Satan can produce an ungodly appetite or thirst, but an appetite or thirst for ungodly things can never be wholly satisfied. Some people search after things in the world, and their search becomes intensified, but they are never satisfied. If we pursue sin, we will never be satisfied. It will end in death, but it will never fulfill us because there is no fulfillment in sin. Fulfillment is found only in Jesus. There is an *object* of the intense ongoing gnawing cry, the desperate need, that we experience within us as a result of the work of the Holy Spirit. The object is righteousness. "He that hungereth...after *righteousness*..." The Greek word translated "righteousness" is *dikaiosune*, and is defined as "the character, or the quality of being right, good, or just."

Matthew 5:20 states, "I say unto you that except your righteousness shall exceed the righteousness of the scribes and Pharisees ye shall in no case enter into the kingdom of heaven." Jesus referred to the righteousness of the scribes and Pharisees, who had established a code in an attempt to satisfy certain moral and ethical standards. In a very real sense of the word, that is a form of self-righteousness, and any group can define a code which could be considered self-righteousness. Some codes are at a higher moral and ethical level than others, but Jesus was revealing something important by referring to the scribes and Pharisees. These men were practicing the highest moral and ethical level of righteousness developed by human beings at that time. However, the highest level of human self-righteousness falls far short of the righteousness of God.

God Is Righteousness

Isaiah 64:6 declares, "We are all as an unclean thing, and our righteousness is as filthy rags. And we all do fade as a leaf; and our iniquities, like the wind, have taken us away." Our righteousness, which may be impressive in our sight, is not impressive in God's sight. There is no way that humans can produce a code of righteousness that is like the Lord's. Where then is our hope? Our hope is in seeing the righteousness of God. When Jesus speaks of righteousness, He's not speaking about an <u>action</u> of God, but rather an <u>attribute</u> of God. It isn't that God just does righteous things, which of course He does, but it is that God <u>is</u> righteousness. You cannot separate the attribute from the person. If you're going to have the righteousness of God you must take God, and if you take God then you get the righteousness of God. Righteousness is an attribute of God.

In I Corinthians 1:30, Paul said about Jesus Christ that "<u>He is made unto us</u> wisdom and <u>righteousness</u> and sanctification and redemption." The very essence of God's being is righteousness. If God is righteousness, and I seek after righteousness, then by definition I seek after God. Another interpretation of this principle could be: "They that hunger after the fullness of God, all that God is, the presence of God and the person of God....shall be filled." (This subject is addressed in greater detail in our book, *Bread that Satisfies).* We have become acclimated to seeking after what God <u>does</u> rather than who God <u>is</u>. Our prayers are often, "Bless me, feed me, change me, touch me." We tend to seek after what He does, while He desires that we seek after who He is. The joy is in the fact that when we get <u>Him</u>, we get everything He does and also everything He has. You've heard it said, "Don't seek healing, but rather seek the healer." That means when we have the healer, we not only have healing, but we have health.

A Desperate Craving for God

Jesus is teaching us that the Holy Spirit will create in us a craving and desperation for God until we are dissatisfied with anything less. I believe that once we have a genuine encounter with Him, we will never be satisfied with religion again. There is something about the presence of the Lord that is fulfilling and satisfying. (Psalm 16:11) We must understand this principle, because this is the difference between people that are simply involved in religious activity and those that are empowered from on high.

Where is the power of God? The power of God is in God, and when He is in us, so is His power. Jesus is communicating the importance of understanding that spiritual life, satisfaction, and fulfillment can only be experienced in His person. In the same way that we cannot sustain life in our physical bodies without an outside source of food or water, it is likewise true in a spiritual sense. Jesus said, "I am the bread of life." (John 6:35) He didn't say, "I give the bread of life," such that we would run to Him at least three or four times a week to get a loaf. That's religion. There's a higher way than running to Him and getting a loaf, and that higher way is understanding that when we receive Him, we have bread as a continual supply.

Chapter 4 of the Gospel of John speaks of a woman who went to Jacob's well every day with her bucket. That was her lifestyle. A bucket full, another bucket full, and another bucket full. The man at the Gate Beautiful (Acts 3:1-10) was asking alms everyday, day after day. He was going from basket to basket, even as she was going from bucket to bucket, simply surviving. Peter said, "Such as I have, give I unto thee. In the name of Jesus Christ of Nazareth, rise and walk." The man leaped to his feet and ran into the temple glorifying God. What did he have now? He had Jesus; he didn't just have a basket full. The woman at the well ran with excitement into the city. What did she have now? She had Jesus; she didn't just have a bucket full. During her lifetime, there were six men who had played significant roles in her life - five husbands plus the man who was currently in her life - but none of these six men brought fulfillment to her heart. Jesus was the "seventh man," and when she met Him, everything changed. Jesus effectively said, "I'm not here to fill your bucket. I'm here to eliminate your need for a bucket and give you water whereby you will never need to run to the well again. I'm going to fulfill you, complete you, and satisfy you. I'm not just one more man; I'm the Son of God. I'm going to change your life."

Jesus Is Everything

In a very practical sense it's not so much about us getting more of Jesus as it is about Him getting more of us. We must get the clutter out of us that hinders Him from filling and occupying us completely. He is everything. He is the fullness of God. The question is, "How much do we really want Him?" Is it a matter of survival? Have we come to the place where we can't live without Jesus? If we have, that's the result of the Holy Spirit moving in our lives. That's a hunger that is absolutely supernatural. He is the joy and the sustaining power of our lives. As the Holy Spirit increases our hunger for Him, He is ushering us into the place of increased satisfaction and wholeness.

Jesus said that we are very fortunate when we have a craving desire for Him and the fullness of His presence, because we are going to be fulfilled and satisfied. I've served the Lord for all of my knowing years, and I can honestly say I love Him more now than ever before. Some may think that after seventy years of serving God, one may become bored. I disagree. You can't become bored with Jesus. You can become bored with religion very quickly, but not with Jesus. His mercies are fresh every morning. You are highly favored when the Holy Spirit is creating a longing, a desire, and a cry in your heart for Jesus because it's prelude to an ever increasing fulfillment. It's not only a case of submitting to activity, talking about Jesus, or singing about Him; it's a case of enjoying and experiencing Him more and more. This results in a lifestyle of communion and fellowship with Him. It's talking and walking with the One that is living in me and is the very essence of my life.

Some time ago I heard a story of a father who gathered his children together everyday at the dinner hour and instructed one of them to assign the seats. To another, he said, "It's your assignment to set the table." To another, "It's your assignment to bring the centerpiece." At the appointed hour they would all come and sit in their seats, with the table set but with no food on the table. The father would stand and speak to them about how wonderful steak and French fries taste. Then he would get the cookbook and read several pages from it. Then they would all stand and sing a song about ice cream and strawberries. Day after day this scenario would be repeated. One day as they finished this routine, one of the boys raised his hand and said, "Dad, this all sounds good, but I'm hungry." The rest of them turned and looked at him in horror, and said, "What a fanatic!" A few days later when they gathered together, this same son showed up late. He ran in, pulled his chair up to the table, raised his hand, and said excitedly, "Dad, I took a walk today, and at the house down the street I ate some steak, French fries, ice cream, and strawberries, and I want to tell you they are everything you said they are, and more!" Having dared to do that, he was excommunicated by the family.

Jesus is more than someone to talk about, more than someone to sing about. He's someone to enjoy. Blessed are they that hunger and thirst after righteousness, for they shall be filled. Are you hungry?

Chapter 6

Blessed Are the Merciful

"Blessed are the merciful; for they shall obtain mercy." The New American Standard Bible uses the word "receive" rather than "obtain." Therefore, we can interpret this verse as, "Blessed are the merciful; for they shall <u>receive</u> mercy." The New International Version uses the phrase "be shown." "Blessed are the merciful for they shall <u>be shown</u> mercy." This is the first Beatitude we have encountered in which both the condition and the provision refer to the same thing. Up until now, the *condition* spoke to one thing and the *provision* spoke to another. However, the *condition* and *provision* now speak to the same thing - mercy. "Blessed are the merciful; for they shall obtain mercy."

The Law of Reciprocity

This Beatitude contains a beautiful illustration of one of the principle laws of the Kingdom of God, which scholars refer to as "the law of reciprocity." This principle means that there is a direct correlation between what is given and what is received. In addition to referring to mercy in this teaching, Jesus illustrated the principle of reciprocity in many of His other teachings on topics such as judging, forgiving others, and giving and receiving. For example, Jesus said, "Judge not, and ye shall not be judged:

condemn not, and ye shall not be condemned: forgive, and ye shall be forgiven: that ye be not judged." (Luke 6:37) This is an illustration of the law of reciprocity.

Mercy

Mercy is a very important attribute of God, just like love, grace, compassion, long suffering, tenderness, and goodness. All genuine mercy has God at its source, but mercy can be expressed through us because He has deposited it in us. Mercy is not simply something we admire in God, but it is also something we experience and appreciate in ourselves. Most importantly, God meant mercy to be something which we extend and minister to others. So, it starts _with_ Him, it comes _to_ us, and it comes _through_ us to bless others.

The Scriptures speak of the mercy of God. Isaiah 37:26 declares, "He (God) is ever merciful." The mercy of God never runs out. It is new and fresh every morning, like a fountain that is inexhaustible and which flows endlessly. As the life of God is ever present and ever manifested, so is the mercy of God.

Ephesians 2:4 states, "God is rich mercy." So we not only see that He is ever merciful in the extent of time quantitatively (it is never exhausted), but also qualitatively it is rich, deep, valuable, and good. Therefore, it is without end and also abundant and rich. This describes the two dimensions of the mercy of God. He gives mercy to us so that we can begin to appreciate it, understand it, and apply it. We knew very little about the mercy of God until He showed it to us and He told us that He was merciful. He told us that His mercy was going to reach out to us and bring us to Himself, but He had to help us to understand that so that we would appreciate it.

The Mercy Seat

When God gave the specifications for the tabernacle, He specified that there was to be a veil, and behind the veil, a room called the Holiest of Holies. This room was only to be entered on a specific day of the year (the Day of Atonement) by a specific person (the High Priest). When the High Priest entered the Holiest of Holies, he would offer atonement first for his own sins, and then for the sins of the people. God said this would be accomplished using the one and only piece of furniture (the Ark of the Covenant) that He specified to be placed in the Holiest of Holies. The Ark was a box made of acacia wood and overlaid with gold.

Three items were to be placed within the Ark: the tablets of stone containing the Ten Commandments (the Law), Aaron's rod that budded, and a pot of manna. God looked down upon the Ark and saw the Law with its demand for holiness and righteousness, and, because man could not meet that standard (its demand for judgment), God chose to put a covering on top of it, called the mercy seat, with cherubim on either side of the mercy seat. The high priest entered the Holiest of Holies once a year and sprinkled the blood of a bull and a goat on the mercy seat for an atonement for sin. The word "atonement" means "a covering for sin" because the demand for holiness and righteousness could not be met other than through this foreshadow and type of that which was to come and ultimately be fulfilled in Jesus Christ. God said something very powerful to Moses: "I will commune with you between the cherubim." What was between the cherubim? The mercy seat!

God was effectively saying, "The mercy seat will be My throne, and I will commune with you there. You will know Me and I will know you in the place of My mercy." Scripture teaches that the blood of bulls and goats cannot remit sin (Hebrews 10:4); it can only temporarily cover sin. The blood of animals was a foreshadow which looked forward to the great and final sacrifice when the Lamb of God shed His blood. His blood would be put on the mercy seat forever.

When Jesus died on the cross and shed His blood, He dealt with the demands of the law and the requirements for righteousness and holiness. Romans 3:25 states that He was made a propitiation for us, which means that His sacrifice satisfied God's demand for justice. God the Father was satisfied in the shedding of the incorruptible, uncontaminated blood of the Lamb of God. Everything that was demanded was met. It was complete; it was finished!

The offering of the high priest on the mercy seat, set forth hundreds of years before Christ, helps us to appreciate the mercy of God. If we remove the mercy, there is nothing left but a demand for judgment. However, mercy provides us with a place to commune with God. We need His mercy because we can never satisfy the demands of the law ourselves, regardless of how good a moral life we have lived. Isaiah 64:6 declares, "We are all as an unclean thing, and our righteousnesses are as filthy rags; and we all do fade as a leaf; and our iniquities, like the wind, have taken us away."

We must understand that God has not compromised His position regarding sin, nor has He said that sin isn't as sinful as it used to be. Sin is just as ugly, horrible, and death-demanding as it ever was, but God has provided a way to satisfy the demands of our failure and to lift us in His holiness and clothe us in His righteousness. It is because of His mercy. Each morning when we awaken, at the very least we should thank Him for His mercy, which is fresh every morning. (Lamentations 3:23) If God hadn't initiated mercy toward us, we would have remained hopelessly lost. There's no way any of us could ever draw near to Him except that He has made a way by reaching out to us by His mercy.

Chesed and Eleos

To learn more about mercy, we will examine the Hebrew and Greek words from which the word "mercy" is translated, and then derive a composite definition of the word mercy. The Hebrew word is *chesed*, and it means "to get inside the other person's skin until we can see things with their eyes, think things with their mind, and feel things with their feelings." That is exactly what God did in Christ. God manifested Himself in the flesh, yet He did not sacrifice His divinity or compromise His perfection even for a moment.

Hebrews 4:15 declares that our true High Priest (Jesus) is "touched with the feeling of our infirmities." When God came to earth in Jesus Christ, He "crawled into our skin." He knows what it means to be hungry, thirsty, and tired. He knows what it means to be tempted by the enemy, persecuted, oppressed, blasphemed, and falsely accused. Our struggles are not an external concept or abstract theory to Him. Jesus was here and He experienced them. He knows how we feel!

The Greek word for "mercy" helps us to further understand the definition. The noun form is *eleos*, and its adjective form, *eleemon*, is used in Matthew 5:7. It means to be "actively compassionate." Many people do not understand the huge difference between the human emotions of pity and sympathy, and the divine energy of compassion. Compassion, like mercy, emanates from God. It is a divine energy and not simply identification with someone's misfortune or a willingness to listen to their problems. Compassion involves more than saying, "I feel your pain," or "I care about you." Compassion is such a total identification with someone and their need that it expends, involves, and commits itself. The energies of compassion and forgiveness are released by mercy. Because of mercy, compassion is released to the needy and the suffering. Because of mercy, forgiveness is released to the repentant.

Compassion is not a personality trait. It is true that some people appear to naturally be more merciful than others, while some people's personalities seem to be rather harsh. However, when we speak of compassion, we are not speaking of a human attribute, something biological, or something that has been part of our personality from birth. *Compassion is a divine deposit of God.* Compassion is a divine energy and, like love, whenever it is released, something happens! I'm blessed when I read scriptures in the Bible such as, "Jesus had compassion on them, and He healed them." Or, "...and He fed them." Or, "...and He set them free." There is a blessing that always results when compassion is released.

Divine Compassion

Have you ever experienced a divine stirring in your heart for someone you didn't know, or perhaps knew only superficially? Perhaps suddenly the compassion of the Lord came over you and there was something that cried out within you to minister to that person's need. This is the kind of condition to which the Hebrew and Greek words are referring. The Greek word *eleos* links mercy to compassion, and the Hebrew word *chesed* speaks of total identification.

I am in awe of a God that looks down on this mass of fallen humanity and says, "I will give My best to redeem them, restore them, and reconcile them to Myself." What causes Him to do it? Mercy! Mercy isn't reactionary, and it doesn't look to help someone in order to receive something in return. *Mercy has nothing to do with "what you can do for me" and everything to do with "what I can do for you."*

"Blessed are the merciful." What does this mean? When we become merciful, it means the Holy Spirit is "tampering" with our lives, and this divine energy is beginning to be released through us. When that happens, there is a double blessing involved. Not only are those to whom mercy is flowing helped and strengthened, but mercy also comes back to the giver of mercy, because Jesus said that the merciful shall receive mercy. It is wonderful to give something away that we can't lose! We give mercy away and yet we still have it. This has to do with the fact that mercy originates with God, and it's rich and inexhaustible. We are doubly blessed because God wants us to be a dispenser of that incredible mercy. The God of mercy is living in us! His mercy will reach the unreachable, touch the untouchable, love the unlovable, and redeem the lost.

Three Attributes of Mercy

I believe that Jesus spoke of three attributes of God's mercy in the "Parable of the Good Samaritan" in Luke Chapter 10. He whose attribute is mercy not only manifested and demonstrated it, but He also defined it for us. In the parable, Jesus spoke of three people who crossed the path of a needy person. Jesus asked His hearers, "Which now of these three, thinkest thou, was neighbour unto him that fell among the thieves? And he said, He that shewed mercy on him." (Luke 10:36-37a) The Greek word translated mercy there is *eleos*. It's the noun form of the same word that is found in adjective form in Matthew 5:7. Jesus said that the one that showed mercy on the hurting man was _truly_ his neighbor.

Attribute #1: See the Need and Identify With It

Jesus then said to His listeners, "Go, and do thou likewise." (Luke 10:37b) It is clear that Jesus wasn't simply telling a story to which we should listen and reflect upon. Rather, He was revealing something so we will become involved. He was teaching that mercy is not simply to be admired, but to be practiced and to become a part of our daily lives and our character. How did the man in the parable show mercy? *The first attribute of mercy is to see the need and identify with the hurting*.

Luke 10:30 states, "And Jesus answering said, A certain man went down from Jerusalem to Jericho, and fell among thieves, which stripped him of his raiment, and wounded him, and departed, leaving him half dead."

Please note the word "thieves." We can glean a spiritual truth by understanding that Satan is a thief. Jesus spoke of Satan when He said, "The thief cometh not, but for to steal, and to kill, and to destroy." (John 10:10) Therefore, this parable is referring to situations, people, nations, cities, and families that have been robbed and stripped by Satan. Jesus cares about the needs of all people. I believe, in these last days, we are going to experience an increasing concern and compassion for people that are in need. We have not been called to pursue a lifestyle where we are on a track to heaven and isolated from the needs of others. The track on which Jesus has His Church runs directly through the middle of the world, through broken lives, broken hearts, broken homes, and broken families. I believe that the church of Jesus Christ is going to become very involved in the ministry of restoration in this end time hour. We must realize it will not be "out of the ordinary" to encounter people that have been robbed and stripped by Satan. Most of us encounter them on a daily basis at home, at work, or in our neighborhoods, literally almost everywhere we go. I wonder how many of them we simply pass by every day?

Jesus continued with the parable, "By chance there came

down a certain priest that way; and when he saw him, he passed by on the other side." Scholars have debated the reason that the priest passed by the hurting man. Theories include he was too busy being religious, or that he felt there was no hope, or that he didn't really want to identify with such a mess. "And likewise a Levite, when he was at the place, came and looked on him, and passed by on the other side. But a certain Samaritan, as he journeyed, came where he was, And when he saw him, he had compassion on him."

The first thing the Samaritan did was go to the hurting man. The other two saw the same man, the same mess, but they passed by. One of the attributes of mercy is to see the need, and to identify with it. The Samaritan saw the need for mercy and was drawn to it. He may have thought, "I can't go on with my life today until I do something about that." I believe that the Samaritan saw the same physical scene as the other two men, yet he "saw" it differently than they did. The other two had seen him as half dead, but the Samaritan saw him as half alive. Perhaps the other two thought, "If I leave him alone he'll die" while the Samaritan may have thought, "I can do something so that he'll live."

So the Samaritan went to the hurting man and identified with him. He was willing to give his time, strength, resources, and energy, and set aside other plans he had already made, in order to take action to minister to the needy man. I think it's fair to say that the Samaritan climbed into the skin of this wounded man (*chesed*). He felt the man's hurt and his pain. He felt the inability of that man to save himself. He felt the helplessness that man felt. He crawled into his skin and identified with him, which is the first step. But he didn't stop there, because the Bible states that he "bound up his wounds, pouring in oil and wine." He didn't only *observe* the need but he *responded* to the need. He didn't only see it and care about it, but he became actively involved in ministering to it.

Attribute #2: Carry What Is Needed

Where did the Samaritan get the bandages to bind this man up? Where did he get the oil and the wine? Out of his own bag. He had what was needed to minister mercy. There are many things we can carry in our spiritual "bag" (our life) but we must carry oil and wine. Oil is a type (symbolic) of the Holy Spirit, and wine is a type (symbolic) of joy. It's a necessity to have the Holy Spirit as well as the joy of the Lord in our bag when we are "walking in the world" because we don't always have time to go back and replenish them through prayer or worship.

Thankfully, the Samaritan didn't have to look at the mess and say to the man, "Hang in there while I go and obtain what you need." Thankfully, he didn't scribble down someone else's address and say, "Contact this person. They have oil and wine. They will be able to help." The Samaritan was prepared to minister to the man with what was needed at that very moment. Like the Samaritan, we must allow God to place oil and wine in each of our bags. You may think you do not have much oil or wine, but when you begin to give what you have, God can work wonders in the lives of others. Give what you have and watch what God will do with it!

A God that can feed thousands with two loaves and five fish can take what is in you and make it enough. I'm not suggesting that we should be slothful or unprepared. Indeed, we should prepare ourselves to minister to others daily through prayer, Bible study, and personal times of devotion and worship. We should never disqualify ourselves for ministry by concluding that we don't have anything to meet the need. If the Samaritan would have reached that conclusion, the wounded man likely would have died. Instead, he lived! We haven't been called to stand back and complain about what a mess this world is in, or lament that we are powerless to do anything. We're in this world, on this "Jericho Road," for a purpose. I must believe that no matter how bad a mess in which someone finds themselves, they can live!

I recall a man who approached me following a church service a number of years ago grinning from ear to ear. He said, "Pastor I never had a chance to give you my testimony. For fourteen years I was hopelessly addicted to drugs and my family was in shambles. I started going to church. God saved me and delivered me instantaneously from my addiction, and my life changed overnight!" We must dispel the notion that some "messes" are impossible to clean up. We should never look at any mess and think that the only hope is death. Regardless of the mess God may allow us to encounter, we have the responsibility to believe for life and not death! We must bind the wounds and pour the oil and wine.

Attribute #3: Commit Until the Job is Done

Mercy is not simply identifying with a need, or getting involved, but also committing unreservedly, and the Samaritan did that very thing. He set the wounded man on his own beast. The Samaritan "gave up his own ride," took the man to an inn, and took care of him. Luke 10:35 states, "And on the morrow when he departed, he took out two pence, and gave them to the host, and said unto him; Take care of him; and whatsoever thou spendest more, when I come again, I will repay thee."

Often, staying committed until the job is done is the hardest part of being merciful. We tend to grow impatient when things don't progress as quickly as we would like. We may feel that we are expending too much time, energy, or resources, on one person or situation. We may become lazy or selfish in our thinking. Perhaps we started out well, but we don't feel like following through. True mercy sometimes involves pouring out more than one bottle of oil or wine. We should not give up, because God never gave up on us. His mercy doesn't run out. His mercy remains and is rich. Our biggest problem is our human emotion and our flesh. We can tend to become weary, impatient, or distracted too quickly.

I want to encourage you if you have become frustrated or discouraged while praying for someone, helping someone, or working with someone over a period of time. Perhaps you feel that the situation is getting worse instead of better. You must be careful not to simply conclude from the outward appearance that they are not going to make it.

Go and Do Likewise

I believe the Lord is calling His people today to walk in mercy, and mercy is needed like never before as we observe the condition of our world. Jesus showed us which of the three showed mercy - the Samaritan. Why? Because the Samaritan got involved and wouldn't give up. He stayed with it and he gave everything that was needed. If the story ended there, we would simply have a beautiful Sunday school lesson...except Jesus has one more thing to say to us. "Go and do thou likewise." That is more difficult, because it requires effort on our part.

At my age, it is easy to sit in the bleachers watching youngsters playing sports, notice their mistakes, and point out the things they could do better. But please don't ask me to put on a uniform and get into the game...that is much more difficult! Likewise, in our Christian walk, we can sometimes sit back and become spectators rather than participators in God's plan of mercy and ministry. He has called us to get involved! We must always keep in mind that it is not our human ability, intelligence, or education that qualifies us. What truly matters is that the God of mercy lives in us. Our mission is to release the Spirit through us and allow His mercy to flow.

God effectively said to Moses, "You will know I am alive and see Me in My glory and power. You will find Me between the cherubim on the mercy seat." That's how we enter God's presence today - through Jesus Christ our mediator, intercessor, advocate, and our mercy seat. The mercy of God manifest through Jesus Christ has been deposited in us and must be demonstrated through us that He may be glorified.

A Prayer for Mercy

Lord, I pray that You will give us an increasing appreciation of Your mercy. We realize that we cannot really know mercy except we experience it first from You, and then allow it to flow through us to others. I pray for the people that are hurting, wounded, weary, distressed, and heavy laden. God, reveal Your glorious mercy to them. Let them know that You have identified with our needs, and You understand our situation.

Lord, I pray if anyone reading this feels like a failure or wants to give up, that You will draw them to Yourself by Your mercy. Let them know that You will hear as they call upon Your name. As they bow before You, they will receive Your love because Your mercy is inexhaustible. It's rich, unending, and fresh every day.

Lord, I pray for all of us who are called to be merciful. I pray You will help us to see that You have deposited everything that is needed in us. Help us to begin to move in mercy, identifying with other peoples' needs, involving ourselves and committing our resources. We credit Your mercy with all that we are and all that we have. We need Your mercy, so we commit to be merciful. We rejoice to know that mercy is greater than judgment, life is greater than death, and hope shines in the darkness. Blessed are the merciful, for they shall obtain mercy.

Chapter 7

Blessed Are the Pure in Heart

Matthew 5:8 declares, "Blessed are the pure in heart for they shall see God." Jesus says that we are fortunate when the Holy Spirit produces purity of heart in us. Why? Because we "shall see God." We are fortunate when we are "pure in heart" (*condition*) for we shall "see God" (*provision*).

The Provision: See God

What did Jesus mean when He said we shall "see God?" The word "see" in the New Testament is translated from several different Greek words, and in the Old Testament, it is translated from more than one Hebrew word. Our natural sight is limited by the location of our eyes, which restricts the arc of our field of vision. For example, because our eyes are on the front of our head, we cannot see what is directly behind us without turning our head. Our sight is limited further in that our eyes don't have the power of a telescope to see great distances or the power of an electron microscope to see minute particles. There are many things that exist that we cannot see without magnification.

Additionally, there are many invisible things that exist which are not "seeable" with the human eye. Even with the most powerful telescope or microscope in the world, we cannot see the invisible. There are realms that exist which cannot be seen by the natural eye. One such invisible being is the person of God Himself. God is very real. He is not a figment of imagination, a product of fantasy, or an object of philosophy. Spirit is substance and God is spirit (John 4:24). He is very real. However, in our natural bodies we cannot physically see Him unless He makes Himself visible to us. How do we see God or hear God? We can do so only when He causes us to see the invisible and hear the inaudible. This is called spiritual vision and spiritual hearing, and this is what Jesus was referring to in this particular Beatitude.

The Greek word that Jesus used for "see" is not limited to the future. The tense of that verb includes the future but also refers to the present. Some people have taken this Beatitude and projected it solely into the future, concluding that "seeing God" means someday we will be able to look upon God's face in heaven. It is indeed true and scripturally accurate to say that we shall behold Him face to face someday. There is coming a fullness of seeing and beholding everything He is. However, we must understand that seeing God is not limited to the future, but also meant for the present. Jesus wasn't speaking to the disciples about seeing God at some point in the future; He was referring to something that applied to them in their "now."

One of our privileges and part of our inheritance as born again believers is seeing God. Jesus told Nicodemus that unless a person is born again, he cannot even see the Kingdom of God. He said we can't see that which is unseeable unless we are born again.

We See God through Jesus

The disciples were struggling with the concept of seeing God. John 14:8-9 states, "Philip said to Him, Lord, show us the Father, and it is enough for us. Jesus said to him, Have I been so long with you, and *yet* you have not come to know Me, Philip? He who has seen Me has seen the Father; how *can* you say, `Show us the Father'?" This exchange occurred near the end of Jesus' earthly ministry, and even at that point, the disciples had only seen a part of what they considered "God." They had spent many months with Jesus, but they were effectively saying, "Jesus, there is only one thing that we lack in order to feel complete - we want to see the Father." Jesus took the opportunity to reinforce the concept of seeing God to which He had introduced them many months earlier through this Beatitude on the mount. He said, "If you have seen me, you have seen the Father."

We understand from studying the Word that when Jesus spoke of seeing Him, He wasn't referring to the physical dimension. He wasn't speaking of His facial features, height, weight, or the color of His hair. In fact, none of the physical attributes of Jesus are even recorded in the Bible. We are such "formula people" that if we knew what Jesus had looked like physically, we could become preoccupied with it and put more emphasis on His appearance than on His person and character. The Holy Spirit carefully recorded in Scripture only those things which are important for us to know. It wasn't Jesus' physical bodily manifestation that He was talking about.

What did Jesus really show the disciples and us? He

showed us the nature and the character of the Father. Many of the "religious people" of Jesus' day had it all wrong. They didn't know who God was. Jesus showed us God when He demonstrated compassion, mercy, love, and grace. Jesus said, "I only do what I see the Father do." Jesus would see what the Father did and then do it so we could "see the Father." Through Jesus, we see the Father. Jesus' character, nature, and actions demonstrate the Father's character, nature, and actions.

The first way through which the Father chose to show Himself to us is through His Son, Jesus Christ. However, many people, even "religious people," didn't see Him that way. The Pharisees, Scribes, and Sadducees called Jesus a blasphemer because they didn't see God when they saw Jesus. Jesus called them blind and said they had eyes yet couldn't see. This principle is still true today. We cannot see God except through Jesus Christ. Jesus is the door. He is the way and the truth. We cannot see God through philosophy, education, or religion. We can only see Him through Jesus.

We See God through His Word

Secondly, God chose to show Himself to us through His Word. John 1:1 declares, "In the beginning was the Word, and the Word was with God, and the Word was God." This verse is speaking of the living Word, Jesus Christ. "In Him was life; and the life was the light of men. And the light shineth in darkness; and the darkness comprehended it not." (John 1:4-5) However, He has also revealed and manifested Himself through the written

Word, the inspired Word of God. The word "inspired" means "breathed from God." God exhaled and the Word came out. If we want to know God, we must know His Word, the Bible. We must study and know the Word, live the Word, and breathe the Word. He exhaled the Word that we might inhale the Word. *We can "see God" through His Word, the Bible.*

We See God through His People

Thirdly, God chose to reveal Himself to us through other born again believers. He said our bodies are the temple of the Holy Spirit. (I Corinthians 6:19) He moves into us that He might manifest Himself through us - born again believers. Therefore I can see God in you, and you can see God in me. Unfortunately, many people only look for and see other people's failures, faults, weaknesses, and mistakes, and therefore they never see God through others. If we look at others and focus on the great things that God has deposited in them, we can see God in them!

The Condition: Pure In Heart

There is a condition to seeing Him, and this condition determines to what extent we see Him. Paul wrote about seeing through a glass darkly. (I Corinthians 13:12) If someone who wears eyeglasses never cleans them, everything looks dirty and they cannot see clearly. The clarity of our spiritual sight is a function of the condition of our purity of heart. The Holy Spirit desires to produce purity of heart in us because God wants us to see Him in His glory, majesty, beauty, power, grace, love, and mercy. Who can describe His beauty? To some He's lovely. To others He's wonderful. To others He's beautiful. To others He's indescribable. Purity of heart is the condition which must be satisfied in order to truly see God.

Pure = Without Spot and Without Wrinkle

"Blessed are the pure in heart." The word pure in the Greek is *katharos* and speaks of two distinct things. First it means to be clean, not only in the sense of "without spot" but also to be "finished." In Hebrew custom, though a soiled garment had been washed, it was not considered completely clean until it was pressed and had no wrinkles. In the Hebrew, the word pure not only means "without dirt" but it also means "without wrinkle." It's interesting that this is touched upon in Ephesians 5:27 where Paul writes, speaking of Jesus, "That he might present it to himself a glorious church, not having spot, or wrinkle, or any such thing; but that it should be holy and without blemish."

First, the cleansing process in us begins with the cleansing agent of the blood of Jesus Christ. The only agent to cleanse sin is the blood of Jesus. We cannot begin to see God at all until the blood of Jesus has been applied to our hearts, and we've been born again. I Corinthians 2:14 declares, "But the natural man receiveth not the things of the Spirit of God: for they are foolishness unto him: neither can he know them, because they are spiritually discerned. " Until we are born again, we can create a mental image of God, but we cannot see God.

Secondly, this process of ironing out the wrinkles occurs through the work of the Holy Spirit and the Word of God. Paul tells us in Ephesians 5:26 that we are cleansed by the washing of water by the word, so the Word of God is a cleansing agent. The Word of God can iron out wrinkles in our lives. Sometimes we may begin to think our "garment" is in pretty good shape, but the Word of God reveals to us that we need to iron out a wrinkle or two. We have an ongoing purifying agent. I John 1:9 declares, "If we confess our sins, he is faithful and just to forgive us our sins, and to cleanse us from all unrighteousness." We need the blood, the Word, and the work of the Spirit in the purifying process.

Pure = Unmixed

The word pure in the Greek and Hebrew not only carries the meaning of "cleansing," but also "to be unmixed." For example, milk that was diluted with water in Biblical times was called "impure milk." Similarly, after the chaff was removed from the corn, it was called "pure corn." God reduced Gideon's army to three hundred men by telling the men that were fearful to go home. He purified the group by removing the mixture. The Children of Israel encountered difficulty in the wilderness because they left Egypt with a mixed multitude. Mixture is always a problem because that which is foreign (not of the same substance or nature) ruins the purity. Being pure in heart means to have nothing hidden; to have no deception, double mindedness, or double vision. We are called to be singly focused on God. We cannot look in two directions at the same time. Jesus taught this principle throughout the Word. He said no man can serve two masters, yet people still try. Jesus said that it is a mixture and it is impure.

Going Nowhere

Pursuing a path of double mindedness or double vision will hinder us from seeing God in His beauty, majesty, glory, and holiness. The extent to which we see Him is determined by the extent to which our hearts are pure before Him. Our hearts must be clean and not mixed. James 4:8 declares; "Cleanse your hands, ye sinners; and purify your hearts, ye double minded." James 1:8 states, "A double minded man is unstable in all his ways." Being double minded means that we vacillate. "I think I will, I think I won't, I think He will, I'm not sure He will. I'm sure that's what it says, I'm not sure it does. I think I'll serve Him, I'm not so sure." We can become weary because of our vacillating because we are not growing in spiritual maturity. We are "going nowhere fast."

When I played little league baseball, there was a boy on our team that was very slow afoot. Our coach used to tell him that he would be fast if he didn't run so long in the same place. That's what double mindedness is like - running in place. We get worn out and never get anywhere. We must make up our mind that we are going to serve the Lord and seek the will of God. There are certain things we must settle. "...Purify your hearts, ye double minded." (James 4:8) "A double minded man is unstable in all his ways." (James 1:8) We must settle on the fact that Jesus is Lord, that we will believe His Word, walk in it, and live by it. People are surprised how the Word opens up to them once they settle on the fact that it is truly God's Word. The reason the Word isn't alive to a lot of people is that they haven't settled that in their mind.

The Word of God Coming Alive

I have had people say to me, "I don't understand why the Word isn't alive to me." I believe it has a great deal to do with how we approach the Word and what we believe about the Word. If I believe that the Bible is the Word of God, He can open it up to me because I'm not going to violate it. I am going to cherish it and consider it precious. The purity and single mindedness by which I approach the Word has a great deal to do with how I see God in His Word. Someone may say, "I don't understand why I don't receive from the Word." Jesus said, "You shall live by every word that proceeds out of my mouth." If we are unwilling to accept and believe every word, we will not see God.

From the Inside Out

"Purify your hearts ye double minded." "....Unite my heart to fear thy name." Psalm 51:10 declares, "Create in me a clean heart, O God, and renew a right spirit within me." Why does God put so much emphasis on the condition of the heart? After all, that's a part none of us can see. We focus more on our outward appearance and reputation. However, if we study the Word, we will learn that everything God does is from the inside out, from the invisible to the visible. Before the visible kingdoms of this world existed, the invisible Kingdom of God already existed, and will always exist. Someday, the Kingdom of God will swallow up all the kingdoms of the world. (Revelation 11:15) The visible things we see in this world will only last for a short period of time. Some people have anchored their entire life in the visible things which will soon pass away.

Matthew 12:34 Jesus said; "....Out of the abundance of the heart the mouth speaketh." We can concentrate on learning a new vocabulary or memorizing a certain theology or philosophy, but that which comes out of us is only as effective and powerful as that which is in us. That's why Jesus is concerned about purity of heart.

Proverbs 23:7 states, "As a man thinketh in his heart, so is he." Proverbs 4:23 declares, "Keep thy heart with all diligence; for out of it are the issues of life." God is putting His finger on the thing that is really important to Him. We spend so much time trying to work from the outside in, when God is saying, "If you'll let Me work by My Holy Spirit on the inside, I'll bring it out." It's not a case of being conformed to some mold or pressure that is put upon us from the outside, but rather being transformed in our spirit such that, as Jesus said, out of our innermost being shall flow rivers of living water. (John 7:38)

Many people have had an experience where they have struggled with a problem or habit that they knew was not pleasing to God, and it really had a grip on their life. They worked on it and every new year they made a resolution to cease doing it. They tried everything and even had people praying for them. Finally, one day they got on their face before

God and said, "Lord, I'm sick of this sin. Please clean me up and change me." They arose and they were different. What happened? The heart got changed, and it changed everything else.

We can summarize this principle in this way: _we are fortunate when our heart is cleansed and unmixed_. If we are single minded and unmixed, we shall witness the beauty, majesty, grace, love, mercy, compassion, glory, and wonder of God. We shall see Him! This kind of seeing is something that sweeps over our whole being and brings a "knowing" that is so all consuming that it is indescribable.

What We Are Affects What We See

Titus 1:15 declares, "Unto the pure all things are pure." Our internal condition affects what we see. Did you ever know anyone that has a "dirty mind?" You can be talking to them and say a simple sentence with all innocence, with no unintended second meaning, and they will interpret it in an "off color" manner. The problem is they're dirty inside, so everything they hear or see is filtered through that dirtiness. They see immorality or evil when it's not intended.

Psalm 24:3-4 declares, "Who shall ascend into the hill of the Lord? Or who shall stand in his holy place? He that hath clean hands, and a pure heart; who hath not lifted up his soul unto vanity, nor sworn deceitfully." No deceit, no vainness, no double mindedness...a pure heart. If we want to see the Lord and know the presence of God in a greater way than we have ever known it before, we must have a pure heart!

Please pray with me. "Lord if there is any impure thing in me, any mixture, please cleanse me. If there is any unconfessed sin, I confess it to You now knowing that You are faithful and just to forgive my sin and cleanse me from all unrighteousness. Wash me in Your Word, O Lord. Iron out every wrinkle in my life, for I want to know You in the fullness of Your presence and Your power. Cleanse me, O Lord, and see if there be in me any unclean or impure thing in me." Blessed are the pure in heart for they shall see God!

Chapter 8

Blessed Are the Peacemakers

Matthew 5:9 declares, "Blessed are the peacemakers; for they shall be called the children of God." Jesus was saying that we are fortunate people when we have the desire to be peacemakers. He didn't say being peaceful, or being lovers of peace...He said "peacemakers." We are fortunate when the Holy Spirit produces a peacemaking heart in us. Why? Because of the wonderful *provision* - we shall be called the children of God. Peacemakers shall be called the children of God!

The Provision: Called Children of God

Some Bible translations use the phrase "sons of God" rather than "children of God." Perhaps that's more accurate because the Greek word *huioi* literally means "sons." Jesus was speaking about relationship, and He was saying when a peacemaking heart exists, we shall be called "the sons of God." He was speaking not only about what God calls us but about what others call us as well.

The phrase "sons of God" is commonly used in the Hebrew language. Adjectives are very rare in the Hebrew language so it is somewhat different than the English language, which uses many adjectives. For example, when we refer to a car, we often use adjectives like large, fast, red, etc. to describe the car. These are descriptive words that help us understand what we mean when we're referring to a car in a particular context.

The Hebrew language is not normally constructed in that manner. When the Hebrew language describes a noun, a phrase such as "sons of God" is sometimes used. For example, Barnabas was called "the son of consolation." (Acts 4:36) So the word "of" is not only attached to a person, it is attached to a thing, in this case "consolation." If we were to say it in English, we would say "a consoling man," or "a comforting man," rather than a "son of consolation." Similarly, the phrase "son of peace" would refer to a peaceful man, with the word "peace" describing the noun "man." Therefore the phrase "a son of God" effectively means "a godly man," or someone that reflects the character of God, and is doing the will of God. Jesus was saying something powerful. He was effectively saying, "Blessed are the peacemakers for they shall be called godly men. They shall be called people that reflect the character of God. They shall be called people that are doing the will of God."

The Condition: Peacemaker

What is the condition that results in us being called a godly man? Let's look at that phrase for a moment, and let's see what the scriptures have to say. As we do, please understand that although the word "man" or "sons" is used, this principle is referring to both male and female.

The word "peace" is a powerful word in Scripture. There

are over four hundred references to peace in the Bible. Every book in the New Testament contains the word peace at least once except I John. We hear this word a lot in our day as well. We hear it as one of the primary objectives of our human race, our society, and our world. However, the Biblical definition of peace is very different than the worldly understanding of peace. It is therefore no surprise to me that many people in the world who are seeking peace have failed to find, attain, possess, experience, and/or manifest it. We will examine both the Hebrew word and the Greek word for "peace" in order to gain a fuller understanding of it.

Peace = the Highest Good and a Harmonious Relationship

The Hebrew word for peace is *shalom*. Jewish people often use that word, and they frequently smile when they say it. There is a very pleasant countenance associated with the word *shalom*, and the reason for that is important. The word *shalom* is never translated in the negative sense. It does not mean to be without trouble. It is not interpreted to mean something that doesn't exist but it is rather interpreted in the positive, and it means, "May everything that makes for your highest good be yours." Therefore, the Biblical word "peace" is intended to send a blessing. It is like saying, "May everything of highest good be yours." Again, it has nothing to do with the absence of trouble, which is the way we typically think of the word peace, like tranquility, meaning there isn't a storm, a conflict, or a war; or everything isn't falling apart. That's not what peace means in the Bible.

The Greek word for peace is *eirene*, which means "a harmonious relationship" or "to be in harmony with another." It does not mean the absence of war, trouble, or strife. It does not refer to the absence of anything; it refers to the presence of something. This is very important because a peacemaker is not a person that ends a war, stops a conflict, or quits fighting. Again, if we put the Hebrew and Greek words together, we find that "peace" in the Bible refers to the positive presence of something. Biblical peace is "to be in harmony with someone" and "to know the highest good that can come unto you."

Peace is the Presence of the Positive

In 1945, the United Nations instituted a mission to keep succeeding generations free from the scourge of war. That statement is actually framed in a negative sense. It effectively says, "If we are successful, there will not be war between nations or peoples in the years to come." More than sixty years later, we still have much conflict throughout the world. Our attempt to achieve peace through human effort has failed because we are looking for the negative. We are effectively saying, "If this nation isn't at war with that nation there is peace" but that's not necessarily true. If someone's son isn't arguing with their daughter, the parents may say they are at peace, but that's not necessarily true. If a husband isn't arguing with his wife, others may think they are at peace, but that's not necessarily true. Why? Two people can stand back to back, cross their arms, and never say a word to one another, and say they're at peace, but they're not at Bible peace. They may be at world peace, at human peace, but they're not at Bible peace. Why? Because it isn't the absence of their arguing or dirty looks, it's the fact that there is no harmony between them. It isn't until they turn and face each other, and hold each other in their arms, that they're at true Bible peace. It's not the absence of the negative; it's the presence of the positive.

This is an important point because we are so oriented to the negative in our society. Our world is so negative that most people have difficulty approaching the Word of God, because the Bible is a very positive book. We usually read a statement like "Blessed are the peacemakers..." and interpret it in the context of our human learning. That's why our minds must be renewed in the Word of God so that we learn to think along spiritual and Biblical lines instead of along worldly lines. That's why Jesus drew His disciples away from the multitude and called them to sit at His feet so He could tell them the way it really is.

A peacemaker, by Bible definition, is not one who avoids trouble, appeases, or passively accepts everything in order to avoid conflict. That is what many people think of when they think of "peacemaker." They see someone that passively goes along with everything and says, "Everything's OK, it's all good. No matter what you do, how you act, or what you say, it's OK. I just don't want conflict." However, in the Biblical sense, they are not a peacemaker; they are a troublemaker.

Peace through Reconciliation

Jesus was not that kind of a peacemaker. Colossians 1:20, in referring to the work of Jesus at Calvary, states, "Having made peace through the blood of his cross..." The blood and the cross did not come through appeasement, or by Jesus passively accepting that which was brought before Him. In the shedding of blood there was opposition. The shedding of blood cost something. The cross cost something.

How did Jesus make peace? Colossians 1:20 continues, "...by him to <u>reconcile</u> all things unto himself." What God did through Christ was actually bring man back into harmony with Himself. We were not at peace with God but rather enemies of God, "at enmity with God" according to Romans 8:7. We were separated and not on friendly terms because sin had stamped its ugly mark on us, and sin cannot be in harmony with God. Sin and God are not harmonious. God is holy and we were sinners, at enmity with God, so something had to be done to bring us together. Jesus didn't come to tell people not to argue with God or try to be religious. There was a whole group of people, the Pharisees, trying to do that. They would dress themselves up and act in a certain way such that they could look like they were on friendly terms with God. Jesus effectively said, "That's not the way to peace. We must deal with sin, and we deal with sin by the blood and the cross." Therefore, when He dealt with sin He made peace. He reconciled us to God.

In Christ Jesus, we are brought back on friendly terms with God. As our sin is remitted, we are reconciled and brought back together in harmony with God. We cannot be in harmony with God other than through Jesus Christ. Sin must be dealt with because sin causes us to be out of harmony. *Through the blood and the cross, Jesus brought us back into harmony with*

God - He has made peace.   We are at peace with God, not because we have a good feeling inside, but because we're on friendly terms with God.   Having true peace has nothing to do with how we feel.   It has everything to do with our relationship to God.   We have been made friends again.   We are in harmony with God.   Sin has been dealt with.

Breaking Down the Wall of Separation

Ephesians 2:14 states, "He is our peace, who hath made both <those that were at enmity> one, and hath broken down the middle wall of partition between us."   In worldly thinking, someone who breaks down a wall couldn't possibly be called a "peacemaker."   Peace doesn't refer to the absence of the broken wall; it refers to the presence of the harmony.

Jesus broke down the wall that separated us from God. Ephesians 2:14-15 continues, "He hath broken down the middle wall of partition.   Having abolished in His flesh the enmity <unfriendliness between us and God>, even the law of commandments contained in ordinances; for to make in himself of twain one new man, so making peace."   This is how He made peace.   He took that which was at enmity, that which was separated and could never be brought together by the works of man, and He broke down the wall by the blood and the cross, bringing the two together and making one out of them.   That is true peace.   He made harmony.   He made the best good that was possible to come to the separated ones (us).   He brought *shalom*, the peace of God.

Jesus said we're fortunate when the Holy Spirit causes

Living in the Favor of God   93 this to happen in our lives because then we're going to be called godly people, people that are exhibiting the character of God and doing the will and the work of God. How then do we as human beings become peacemakers?

First Step: Be at Peace with God

The first thing important to us as individuals in becoming peacemakers is being at peace with God. Until we're at peace with God, we cannot be at peace with one another. We are sinners by nature. We all came from "The Adam's Family." We are storm centers, troublemakers, and problem creators. Some people continue to be those things their entire lives. We can tell where they have been because they leave a trail of strife and trouble in their wake. The problem is in our sinful human nature - we have been cut off, severed, separated.

II Corinthians 5:18 declares, "Now all things are of God, who hath reconciled us to himself by Jesus Christ." That means that He has brought us back on friendly and harmonious terms with God. The blood of Jesus is vital to the work of redemption. It is not about getting a dose of religion so that we don't go to hell. It is so much more than that; it's a relationship issue. By nature, we are enemies ("at enmity") with God because we are sinners. We could not be brought together because by nature we are polar opposites. Therefore, God took upon Himself the form of flesh in Jesus Christ while never ceasing to be God. He became sin for us who knew no sin that the righteousness of God might be made manifest in us. (II Corinthians 5:20)

As we commit ourselves to Him, confess our sinfulness,

make Him our Lord, and put our faith in His finished work, believing that God raised Him from the dead, our sin is remitted and we are brought back into harmony with God. We are, by the Spirit of God, in harmony with God. We are friends with God, not enemies. It is wonderful to be a friend of God. He's the best, most wonderful, and most faithful friend we will ever have. We have been reconciled, brought back on friendly terms with Him. We have been brought to peace with God and we are in harmony with Him.

After His resurrection, Jesus said to His disciples three times, "Peace be unto you." He said it twice during His first encounter with the disciples (when Thomas was absent), and again the next time they were all together. What was He saying to them? He was effectively saying, "By the work that I have done, I reconcile you unto Myself. You and I are now on friendly terms." He wasn't saying "Calm down." He was saying, "I have good news. You and I (you and God) are on friendly terms again. Come feel the wounds in My hands and side. You are on friendly terms with the Father. Every good thing I give it unto you, this blessing of God made manifest. "

Peace is Found in Him

Before His death, Jesus had already told the disciples that in the world they would have tribulation but in Him they would have peace. (John 16:33) Please note that He said in Him and not in the church. The reason He said in Him is because He is the one that has broken down the middle wall. He is the one that reconciled us to God. People may say, "I thought I can find peace in a place or a thing." No, we only find peace in a Person. We can't have peace toward a thing or a place until we have peace in His Person. Many people don't have peace because it's not conditional upon a situation, circumstance, or place.

Many people seek peace as a feeling or an emotional "high." Peace is not a feeling, it's a relationship - it is being reconciled to God. Philippians 4:7 declares, "And the peace of God, which passeth all understanding, shall keep your hearts and minds through Christ Jesus." Peace isn't something we get in our hearts and minds; it's a power that <u>keeps</u> our hearts and minds. It's a right relationship with Him. We're living out of His life, out of Him as our source. The fact that we're reconciled to God will keep our hearts and minds. Jude 24 states, "Now unto him that is able to keep you from falling and to present you faultless before his throne with exceeding great joy." Jude is referring to that which results from our relationship with God. We are peaceful and at peace because we are in harmony with God.

Second Step: Bringing Others to Peace

We have been reconciled to God by Christ Jesus. (II Corinthians 5:18-20) What happens next? "He hath given to us the ministry of reconciliation. To wit, that God was in Christ, reconciling the world unto himself, not imputing their trespasses unto them; and hath committed unto us the word of reconciliation." II Corinthians 5:18 states that we have the <u>ministry of reconciliation</u> and verse 19 declares that we have the word of reconciliation. That is another way of saying that we are called to be peacemakers.

Being a peacemaker means we have been commissioned to bring men, women, boys, and girls back on friendly terms with God. There is so much confusion in the church world about this. Being a peacemaker does not mean that we take a passive attitude and allow someone to become comfortable in their sin. It's not, "You're a peacemaker because you don't disturb me. I'll just continue to commit my habitual sin and you won't say anything against it, so therefore you're a peacemaker." This is not true! In fact, the opposite is true. Anyone who doesn't take a stand against sin is not a peacemaker, but rather a troublemaker! Why? Because sin will destroy that other person and prevent them from being on friendly terms with God. Therefore, as peacemakers, it is our job to tell others that sin will bring death. As a peacemaker it is our responsibility to speak out and do something about sin.

We must understand this truth, because some people think that a Christian who is a "peacemaker" will simply "go along with everything" and try to avoid strife, conflict, and confrontation. That's not peace because it is not bringing someone into reconciliation with God. We must deal with sin. Some people want to live in sin and want every other believer to embrace them and say, "That's OK, everybody has a weakness or falls short somewhere." But that is not peacemaker talk; that's troublemaker talk, because they are not letting the other person know that they are heading toward death. A peacemaker will say, "You must be reconciled to God by the blood of Jesus so that your sin can be cleansed."

Confronting Sin

Paul dealt with the sin of fornication in the church at Corinth. (I Corinthians 5) A man had his father's wife, so Paul rebuked the church, telling them that they were allowing that to continue as if it didn't matter. He said God will judge the world but the church must judge the church. He said it is not OK to allow sin in the church. He told them to put the man out of the congregation. Why? Because Paul was a peacemaker. I have heard people say, "Don't say anything to that person about their sin. Simply love them." However, the best way we can love them is be a peacemaker, and let them know that sin is sin, and that God will judge sin.

There are many people preaching a message in the world that says it doesn't matter what anyone believes, thinks, or acts. They say that it doesn't matter because we're all going to end up in the same place someday. That sounds very "tolerant" and "peaceful" in the ears of most worldly listeners. However, it is really the message of a troublemaker, because it really <u>does</u> matter what we do. The blood of Jesus has remitted our sins. Simply trying to make someone feel good and say, "That's OK," is actually causing them trouble. We are not being kind when we minimize or ignore someone's sin. We should pray for that person and ask God for the words to speak the truth in love to them.

The Ministry of Reconciliation

God has called us to the ministry of reconciliation. Paul was saying the same thing to the Corinthian church that Jesus was saying on the mountain to His disciples. Jesus effectively said that when you're a peacemaker, reconciling people to God, you will be called a godly person. You will be called a person that is displaying the character of God and doing the work of God. "Go ye into all the world and preach the gospel to every creature." What is the gospel, the good news? It is that Jesus has shed His blood and died, paying the price for sin, and we can be reconciled to God. Otherwise we are hopelessly lost. The good news is that we can be on friendly terms with God and come into harmony with Him. This is the greatest way to live. It isn't some kind of a religious experience. It is a relationship - we are on friendly terms! For example, when we see a husband and wife that have been in strife and have not been on friendly terms, but they are now reconciled and on friendly terms, they don't want to live any other way. The only way to live is on friendly terms.

Our mission is to reconcile people to God. Every time we lead someone to the Lord, we are a peacemaker. We are called to be peacemakers, to reconcile men to God. We are not called to make people feel good in their sin. That's actually the worst thing we could do for someone. If I saw you heading over a cliff and I didn't say anything to you except "I love you," would you believe that I love you as you plummet over the edge? No, I don't truly love you unless I say, "Stop!" That's a peacemaker, and that's what Jesus is talking about.

Isaiah 52:7 declares, "How beautiful upon the mountains are the feet of him that bringeth good tidings, that publisheth peace; that bringeth good tidings of good, that publisheth salvation; that saith unto Zion, Thy God reigneth!" One that brings good news is a peacemaker reconciling men to God. Here again is the Hebrew definition of peace, which refers to the best good that can be brought to you.

We Are Called to Be Peacemakers

Jesus said that we are fortunate when the Holy Spirit works in us or uses us to effect right relationship with God because we are reflecting the character of God and doing the work of God, and we will be called a man (or woman) of God. We are fortunate first when the Lord works in us to reconcile us to God, then as a believer when He works through us to effect the reconciliation of others to God, for we are doing the work of God. When we get right down to the simple words of Jesus, that is our call.

I encourage you to tell everyone you know that they can be brought into friendly terms with God. Tell them there's a way to be in harmony with God. Every time a life is transformed and someone is brought back into harmony with God, it will be said that you are a man (or woman) of God, that you are doing the work of God and demonstrating the character of God. You are a peacemaker.

We must pray to become peacemakers, not passive "tolerators" of sin because that will lead people toward destruction. We must deliver the good news that people can be free and in harmony with God. Their life of disharmony and brokenness can be brought back to the way God intended. "He is our peace who hath broken down every wall, and He has taken the twain and made them one." (Ephesians 2:14) He is my peace. Deliver your peace to everybody you meet. Be a peacemaker. Introduce Jesus to people who don't know they can be in right relationship with God. Blessed are the peacemakers!

Chapter 9

Blessed Are the Persecuted

Matthew 5:10-12 declares, "Blessed are they which are persecuted for righteousness' sake; for theirs is the kingdom of heaven. Blessed are ye, when men shall revile you and persecute you, and shall say all manner of evil against you falsely, for my sake. Rejoice, and be exceeding glad. For great is your reward in heaven; for so persecuted they the prophets who were before you." We will consider verses 11 and 12 as one principle because verse 11 speaks the truth in the third person while verse 12 speaks the same truth in the second person.

Jesus said that two *provisions* would result from the *condition* of being persecuted. The first provision is identical to the provision that He gave us in the first Beatitude, namely that we receive the kingdom of heaven (Kingdom of God). The term "Kingdom of God" is synonymous with the term "government of God" which refers to us entering, experiencing, and participating under the rulership of the Lord Jesus Christ and thereby enjoying the blessings of living in His government. We are blessed by the goodness of God that comes through His government. Jesus effectively said that if we seek first the government of God (the Kingdom of God), all of the things that often occupy our thoughts and seem so important will be added to us. (Matthew 6:33) We will realize and experience the things our hearts desire as a consequence of coming under, and walking in, the government of God.

Jesus is speaking again of the invisible world, the Kingdom of God, which is key to our fulfillment, happiness, wholeness, and satisfaction. A beautiful thing about this provision is that He said we will enjoy the greatness of God not only in this life, but also in the future. He said that we should rejoice and be exceeding glad (literally "leap for joy") because great is our reward in heaven. Not only are we blessed in this life, but we can expect the greatness of the reward of God in heaven as well. This Beatitude is very important because it refers to a provision, a great reward, which is eternal - it has no end.

Condition: Persecuted and Reviled

"Blessed are they which are persecuted for righteousness' sake...Blessed are ye when men shall revile you." We are highly favored of God when we are persecuted and reviled.

The verb in the Greek language which is translated to the phrase "which are persecuted" in Matthew 5:10 is in the perfect tense passive voice. This means that it is effective in the past, in the present, and it also has ongoing results. Our verbs in the English language are very limited and are not as expressive as those in the Greek language. English verbs either refer to the past, present, or future. However, Greek verbs have richer meaning, and a single verb can refer to the past, present, and future. That is the verb tense used in this Beatitude. Jesus was saying that this principle, this condition, didn't just come into being when He was here upon the earth but it had existed before, and it would exist into the future. In fact, He used the future tense exclusively in the phrase, "when they shall." (Matthew 5:11) Therefore, Jesus was reaching into the past, present, and into the future.

In the same sense that the *provision* is eternal, the *condition* is also eternal. Therefore, the condition of being persecuted and reviled is relevant to the prophets of old, to the disciples of Jesus' earthly ministry, to us as believers today, and to every believer that follows us on this earth until Jesus comes. This is not a principle which becomes outdated. It is always relevant.

It is important to note that Jesus was not saying that persecution in and of itself is blessed. He was saying that the _reason_ we are persecuted is important. Peter was one of the men on the mountain listening to Jesus teach this principle, and Peter repeated it in his teaching to the church. As recorded in I Peter 4:15-16, Peter referred to the fact that persecution, reviling, evil speaking, and false accusation must be considered in the context of the reason for it. He wrote, "But let none of you suffer as a murderer, or as a thief, or as an evil-doer, or as a busybody in other men's matters." Peter was saying, "Don't tell me that you are 'being persecuted' when you are simply reaping the results of your own wrongdoing." For example, if you are in prison for murdering someone, don't call that "persecution for Jesus' sake." If you have committed a sin or crime for which you are paying the price, don't claim that you are "being persecuted for Jesus' sake." There are situations in life in which we are simply reaping what we have sown and our sufferings have essentially been self-inflicted.

Jesus and Peter were both referring to another kind of suffering and persecution. Peter wrote, "Yet if any man suffer as a Christian, let him not be ashamed; but let him glorify God on this behalf."

Persecuted for Righteousness' Sake

Jesus identified two kinds of conditions which result in persecution and bring the special provision and blessing of God. The first one is in verse 10; "Blessed are they which are persecuted for righteousness' sake." Please note that Jesus didn't say, "Blessed are those which are persecuted...period." He characterized the persecution with the phrase "for righteousness' sake." That means effectively that we are blessed when we are persecuted because we have been acting like Jesus. There is persecution that comes when we act like Jesus would act. For example, when we are honest and don't lie, cheat, or steal, others may persecute us and say things like, "Come on, 'goody two shoes.' Everybody does it."

Jesus was saying that we should not compromise with the ways of the world or the spirit of the world to avoid being persecuted for acting like Him. When we make a decision to act like Jesus, He has a special blessing for us because the principles, truth, power, glory, and majesty of the Kingdom of God favor us. Someone may say, "I'm not sure I can act like

Jesus in this present time." Yes, you can! Will it really work to be honest in business? The Bible says it will and Jesus says it will. Some might say, "But I know people that employ questionable business practices and they seem to end up prospering." However, I would rather have the Kingdom of God supporting me than a temporal prosperity on the part of people whose only measuring stick is worldly affluence. We can't afford not to be doing things Jesus' way. I believe God is bringing the Christian community to the place where we're being challenged by the details of the Word of God. The Word of God is not just a collection of Bible stories; it's a group of principles that work. I believe God is calling us to stand on His principles, live by them, speak them, have faith in them, and know there's no kingdom of this visible world that is greater than the Kingdom of God.

Jesus was saying that there is persecution associated with acting like Him. I Timothy 3:12 declares, "All that live godly in Christ Jesus shall suffer persecution." At some point, someone will probably not feel comfortable because we are living godly in Christ Jesus, and they will persecute us for it. Our alternatives are either to live ungodly and be accepted by the world, or to rejoice in the persecution that results from godly living. Of course, we know which path Jesus desires us to take.

Persecuted For Jesus' Sake

Jesus said that there is a second thing that brings blessing. Matthew 5:11 declares, "Blessed are ye, when men shall revile you, and persecute you, and say all manner of evil against you falsely, for my sake." Some Bible translations use the phrase "because of me" rather than "for my sake." Jesus said a second reason we will be persecuted is effectively "because of Him." When we realize it's because of <u>Him</u> and not because of <u>us</u>, it will affect our attitude. Sometimes we become defensive when persecution comes, and we feel insulted. However, we should not defend ourselves since it is not because of <u>us</u> but rather because of <u>Him</u>.

On the night before His crucifixion, Jesus expounded this truth, saying, "If the world hate you, ye know that it hated me before it hated you. If ye were of the world, the world would love his own; but because ye are not of the world, but I have chosen you out of the world, therefore the world hateth you. Remember the word that I said unto you. The servant is not greater than his lord. If they have persecuted me, they will also persecute you; if they have kept my saying, they will keep yours also. But all these things will they do unto you for my name's sake because they know not him that sent me." (John 15:18-21)

Satan is intimidated and threatened by the Christ in us. If we find ourselves in situations where an ungodly person feels uncomfortable in our company, we must be careful not to take it personally because it's not about us; it's about the Christ in us.

An Example from Peter's Life

The persecution Jesus spoke of comes to us because (1) we act like Him and (2) are identified with Him. We can observe this in Peter's denial of Jesus, recorded in Matthew Chapter 26. If Peter would have listened to Jesus message about persecution more carefully, perhaps he could have avoided this situation. As Jesus was publicly mocked and falsely accused, Peter watched from a distance. Matthew 26:69 states, "Now Peter sat without in the palace; and a damsel came unto him saying, Thou also was with Jesus of Galilee." Peter was being identified with Jesus, but he denied Him. A little while later that same night, Peter denied Jesus a second time. Matthew 26:71 declares, "And when he was gone out into the porch, another maid saw him, and said unto them that were there, This fellow was also with Jesus of Nazareth." These two denials illustrate one of the two reasons for persecution - being identified with Jesus. "Men will revile you, and say all manner of evil against you because of me." (Matthew 5:11)

The other reason for persecution can be seen in Matthew 26:73: "And after a while came unto him they that stood by, and said to Peter, Surely thou also art one of them; for thy speech betrayeth thee." He was persecuted because He was talking like Jesus...Peter was, in effect, acting like Him!

Peter was persecuted first because he was identified with Jesus, and secondly because he was acting like Him. In this instance, Peter shrunk back, pulled back, and fell back. That is not what Jesus wants us to do. Jesus taught that we are not to withdraw or hide because we are to know that there is strength in Jesus Christ. We can be strong and be bold in Him, knowing that the blessings and benefits of the Kingdom of God, as well as the rewards of heaven, are ours as we openly, thankfully, and proudly identify with Jesus and act like Him.

Being Identified with Christ

What is a Christian? First and foremost, the word "Christian" identifies Him, Christ. As Christians, we are identified with a Person rather than actions, religion, or a theological expression. If we are not identified with Him, everything else is "sounding brass, or a tinkling cymbal." (I Corinthians 13:1) As born again believers, we belong to Jesus Christ. Paul wrote, "I am not ashamed of the gospel of Christ for it is the power of God unto salvation to everyone that believeth, to the Jew first, and also to the Greek." (Romans 1:16) Jesus said, "Whosoever therefore shall be ashamed of me and of my words in this adulterous and sinful generation; of him also shall the Son of man be ashamed, when he cometh in the glory of his Father with the holy angels." (Mark 8:38)

When we are identified with Jesus and we act like Him, people may persecute us. Jesus was not saying we should seek persecution, but when it comes we should not shrink from it. We must understand that we will experience persecution if we choose to be identified with Him, act like Him, glorify Him, and live by His Word. People may revile us, defame us, harass us, and possibly even speak evil against us falsely.

One of the most incredible things that can occur in these situations is that the Lord will sometimes take the persecutor with the most hurtful words or the toughest attitude, turn them around, and make them a powerful testimony for His glory. However, if we back down or shrink back from vocal persecutors, how will they see Jesus? They really want what Jesus brings, but they don't yet know it. We are living epistles "known and read of all men" (II Corinthians 3:2) for the joy of being called one of His disciples, one of His people.

A Great Heritage of Believers

In one sense, in the Western world, I'm not convinced we know what persecution really is. There are many written accounts of those that have been persecuted and even killed for the sake of Christ throughout history. We have a great heritage of bold believers who have given their lives for Jesus' sake. One line of the hymn *Onward Christian Soldiers* states, "Brothers, we are treading where the saints have trod." Many great men and women of God have gone before us and have been tremendous examples of the boldness we should have for Christ.

Hebrews 11:36-40 declares, "And others had trial of cruel mockings and scourgings, yea, moreover of bonds and imprisonment: They were stoned, they were sawn asunder, were tempted, were slain with the sword: they wandered about in sheepskins and goatskins; being destitute, afflicted, tormented. (Of whom the world was not worthy): they wandered in deserts, and in mountains, and in dens and caves of the earth. And these all, having obtained a good report through faith, received not the promise: God having provided some better thing for us, that they without us should not be made perfect."

Christians have been burned at the stake and fed to lions for their faith. Emperor Nero of Rome took Christians, dipped them in tar, set them afire, and used them as human torches. Christian tradition tells us that Bartholomew, one of the disciples that heard Jesus teach this Beatitude on the mountain, was flayed (skinned alive). Some believers were torn apart, eyes taken from their bodies.

Persecution can also be verbal, because Jesus said people would say all manner of things against us falsely. Early church history tells us that people were hired and dispatched to slander Christians. Their mission was to find a Christian and lie about them, saying all manner of slanderous things about them. At times, I have been surprised to observe how quickly Christians believe evil reports about other Christians. Perhaps justifiably, we have been accused of slaying our wounded. We owe it to the person about whom we hear an evil report to go to them and find out if the accusation is true. We must understand that the powers of hell are loose to slander Christians. As brothers and sisters in the Lord, we must strengthen, encourage, and defend one another. Our enemy is not one another; our enemy is the satanic powers of darkness.

How Should We Respond?

How should we respond when we are persecuted, reviled, or falsely accused? I Peter 2:20 declares, "For what glory is it, if, when ye be buffeted for your faults, ye shall take it patiently? But if, when ye do well, and suffer for it, ye take it <u>patiently</u>, this is acceptable with God." The key is found in verse 21, "For even hereunto were ye called; because Christ also suffered for us, leaving us an example, that ye should follow his steps." Jesus is our example. What is His example? It can be found in verse 22; "He did no sin." Another way to say that is found in Job 1:22, which states, "In all this Job sinned not, nor charged God foolishly." He didn't become bitter, hurt, resentful, or depressed, which is very easy to do when we are persecuted. Sometimes, we even try to justify ourselves. However, we must remember that our Lord Jesus Christ endured and stood strong and silent before His accusers.

I believe that we are moving into a time of great outpouring of the Holy Spirit, of great revival and great harvest, but there will be opposition. God wants us to be strong in the Lord and in the power of His might. God is not raising a group of weaklings. He is raising up an army of mighty men and women. God is teaching us how to war in the Spirit. "He teacheth my hands to war..." (Psalm 18:34) We know how to fight in the natural. However, we must learn how to fight in the Spirit because our adversary is not flesh and blood, but rather principalities, powers, and rulers of darkness of this world, and spiritual wickedness in high places. (Ephesians 6:12) God is making us strong in the Spirit.

The last part of I Peter 2:22-23 speaks further of Jesus' reaction to persecution when it declares, "...Neither was guile found in his mouth; Who, when he was reviled, reviled not again..." When persecuted, Jesus did not retaliate or try to "get even." Someone once said that the reason some of us never get ahead is that we spend so much time endeavoring to get even. However, when Jesus was reviled, He did not respond in kind.

Notice the last part of verse 23; "...When he suffered, he threatened not; but committed himself to him that judgeth righteously." Jesus prayed and trusted Himself to God. His action said, "I don't have to vindicate myself. God is my protection. He will give me favor. He is on my side." What a wonderful confidence to have! Many of us have tried to vindicate ourselves and only messed up everything! We must know that the Lord is with us, and "if God be for us who can be against us?" (Romans 8:31) He'll fight for us and give us favor with people with whom we could never otherwise gain favor. God will open doors and cause even our enemies to be "at peace" which means to close their mouths.

Jesus amplified this principle, as recorded in Matthew 5:43-45, by saying, "You have heard that it hath been said, thou shalt love thy neighbor, and hate thine enemy. But I say unto you, love your enemies, bless them that curse you, do good to them that hate you, and pray for them which despitefully use you, and persecute you. That ye may be the children of your Father which is in heaven; for he maketh his sun to rise on the evil and on the good, and sendeth rain on the just and on the unjust." We will never really understand the mercy, love, and grace of God this side of heaven, nor will we ever understand why He reaches out, calls, and draws even people like us that don't deserve it!

Matthew 5:46 states, "For if ye love them which love you, what reward have ye? Do not even the publicans the same?" In other words, we don't even have to be spiritual or be a Christian to do that. Jesus continued, "And if ye salute your brethren only, what do ye more than others? Do not even the publicans so?" What a challenge to maturity and wholeness, but the wisdom, strength, power, anointing, love, peace, joy, and favor of

God is released unto us as we do not shrink back from being identified with Him, and as we demonstrate His nature and character by acting like Him.

We must understand that there is no way we can ever imitate Jesus through the power of our human nature. If we try to do this, we will fail. The only answer is to allow <u>the Christ in us</u> to be manifested, unaffected by our emotions, thoughts, or feelings. We all are housed in flesh and have minds that are in the process of being renewed, but we possess within us the Christ of glory. As He is released and allowed to manifest Himself, we will have the strength and wisdom we need to walk in victory each step of the way.

I pray that God will strengthen each of you, because I know there are some who are persecuted in their own home, at their place of employment, in their neighborhood, or in their family gatherings. Jesus is in us to be our strength, help, encouragement, peace, and fortress every moment. We must not shrink from being identified with Jesus or from manifesting His nature and character. We must not allow people to drag us down to their level or convince us that the only way to survive is to follow the ways of the world. As Christians, we know the truth that even after the kingdoms of this world have run their course and have come to an end, the Kingdom of God shall endure from everlasting to everlasting. (Revelation 11:15) Blessed are those who are reviled and persecuted for righteousness' sake!

Chapter 10

Truly Finding God's Favor

God loves you. He wants you to have a personal relationship with Him through Jesus, His Son. There is just one thing that separates you from God. That thing is sin. _The only way to truly live a deeply fulfilling life of favor and blessing is to deal with the sin problem in our lives._

The Bible describes sin in many ways. Most simply, sin is our failure to measure up to God's holiness and His righteous standards. We sin by things we do, choices we make, attitudes we show, and thoughts we entertain. We also sin when we fail to do right things. In short, sin is to miss the mark. The Bible affirms our own experience - "there is no one righteous, not even one." (Romans 3:10 NIV) No matter how good we try to be, none of us does right things all the time.

People tend to divide themselves into groups - good people and bad people. But God says that every person who has ever lived is a sinner, and that any sin separates us from God. No matter how we might classify ourselves, this includes you and me. We are all sinners.

**"For all have sinned and fall short of the glory of God."**
**Romans 3:23(NIV)**

Many people are confused about the way to God. Some

think thy will be punished or rewarded according to how good they are. Some think they should make things right in their lives before they try to come to God. Others find it hard to understand how Jesus could love them when other people don't seem to. But I have great news for you! God DOES love you! More than you can ever imagine! And there is nothing you can do to make Him stop loving you! Yes, our sins demand punishment - the punishment of death and separation from God. But, because of His great love, God sent His only Son Jesus to die for our sins.

"But God demonstrates His own love for us in this: While we were still sinners, Christ died for us." Romans 5:8 (NIV)

For you to come to God you have to get rid of your sin problem. But, in our own strength, none of us can do this! You can't make yourself right with God by being a better person. Only God can rescue us from our sins. He is willing to do this not because of anything you can offer Him, but JUST BECAUSE HE LOVES YOU!

"He saved us, not because of righteous things we had done, but because of His mercy." Titus 3:5 (NIV)

It's God grace that allows you to come to Him - not your efforts to "clean up your life" or work your way to heaven. You can't earn His favor or His salvation. It's a free gift.

"For it is by grace you have been saved, through faith - and this not from yourselves, it is the gift of God - not by works,

so that no one can boast." Ephesians 2:8-9

For you to come to God, the penalty for your sin must be paid. God's gift to you is His Son Jesus, who paid the debt for you when He died on the cross.

"For the wages of sin is death, but the gift of God is eternal life in Jesus Christ our Lord." Romans 6:23(NIV)

Jesus paid the price for your sin and mine by giving His life on a cross at a place called Calvary, just outside of the city walls of Jerusalem in ancient Israel. God brought Jesus back from the dead. He provided the way for you to have a personal relationship with Him through Jesus. When we realize how deeply our sin grieves the heart of God and how desperately we need a Savior, we are ready to receive God's offer of salvation. To admit we are sinners means turning away from our sin and selfishness and turning to follow Jesus. The Bible word for this is "repentance" - to change our thinking about how grievous sin is so that our thinking is in line with God's. All that's left for you to do is to accept the gift that Jesus is holding out for you right now.

"If you confess with your mouth, 'Jesus is Lord,' and believe in your heart that God raised Him from the dead, you will be saved. For it is with your heart that you believe and are justified, and it is with your mouth that you confess and are saved." Romans 10:9-10 (NIV)

God says that if you believe in His Son, Jesus Christ, you can live forever with Him in glory.

"For God so loved the world that He gave His one and only Son, that whoever believes in Him shall not perish but have eternal life." John 3:16

Are you ready to accept the gift of eternal life that Jesus is offering you right now? Let's review what the commitment involves:

- I acknowledge I am a sinner in need of a Savior - this is to repent or turn away from sin.
- I believe in my heart that God raised Jesus from the dead - this is to trust that Jesus paid the full penalty for my sins.
- I confess Jesus as my Lord and my God - this is to surrender control of my life to Jesus.
- I receive Jesus as my Savior forever - this is to accept that God has done for me and in me what He promised.

If it is your sincere desire to receive Jesus into your heart as your personal Lord and Savior, then talk to God from your heart. Here's a suggested prayer: "Lord Jesus, I know that I am a sinner and I do not deserve eternal life. But, I believe You died and rose from the grave to make me a new creation and to prepare me to dwell in Your presence forever. Jesus, come into my life, take control of my life, forgive my sins and save me. I am now placing my trust in You alone for my salvation and I accept your free gift of eternal life."

If you have trusted Jesus Christ as your Lord and Savior, you are now truly able to experience the joy of living in the favor of God! You are truly blessed and highly favored! Spend time with Him each day in prayer and personal worship. Get involved in a local church and serve with all of your heart. God bless you as you enter the exciting new life you are about to experience!

References

Salt for Society
W. Phillip Keller

The Sermon on the Mount
James Montgomery Boice

Studies in the Sermon on the Mount
D. Martyn Lloyd-Jones

About the Author

Blessed with the caring, compassionate heart of a shepherd, Dr. Leonard Gardner has over 55 years of pastoral and ministerial experience. Often called a "pastor's pastor," he has planted churches and mentored pastors and leaders in the true spirit of a "father." Dr. Gardner is the founder of Liberating Word Ministries (www.liberatingword.org) and he travels throughout the United States and abroad with a vision to strengthen and encourage pastors, leaders, churches, and ministries. His heart is for restoration and revival. His style of ministry is seasoned with humor while carrying a powerful anointing. Dr. Gardner has four children and resides in Clinton Township, Michigan with his wife, Rose Ann.

More Inspirational Books from
Dr. Leonard Gardner

Eight Principles of Abundant Living

In this inspiring and thought provoking book, Pastor Gardner examines each recorded miracle in the Book of John to uncover spiritual principles of abundant living which can lead you into a lifestyle of deep satisfaction, joy, fulfillment, and true happiness.

The Unfeigned Love of God

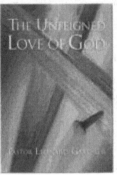

The Bible uses the word "unfeigned" to characterize the indescribable love of God. Unfeigned means "genuine, real, pure, not pretentious, and not hypocritical." This powerful book, derived from a series of sermons by Pastor Gardner, will help you understand, accept, and embrace the incredible love God seeks to lavish on you.

Walking Through the High and Hard Places

Life has its ups and downs. The key to a fulfilling life is learning to "walk through" whatever situation or circumstance you encounter, and to emerge victoriously! The spiritual principles you learn in this book will give you the strength to handle any circumstance in life!

The Work of the Potter's Hands

You are not alive by accident! Isaiah 64:8 declares that God is the potter, and we are the clay. This book examines seven types of Biblical pottery vessels and the process the potter uses to shape and repair vessels. Learn powerful life lessons and know your life is in the hands of a loving God who is forming you through life's experiences so that you "take shape" to fulfill your unique purpose.

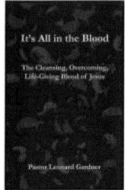

It's All in the Blood

This fascinating book draws intriguing and powerful analogies between the incredible design and operation of blood in the human body, and the life-changing spiritual power and provision that is available in the blood of Jesus Christ.

Like the Eagle

Learn how the eagle's lifestyle and attributes can teach you to "soar higher" in your life, as you become like the eagle in areas such as vision, diet, maturity, renewal, commitment, and living an overcoming life.

The Blood Covenant

Blood covenant is a central theme of the entire Bible, and understanding blood covenant will make the Bible come alive to you in brand new ways. Learn the ten steps of blood covenant, the real significance of communion, the names of God and what they mean, and how walking in a true covenant relationship with God can radically change your life.

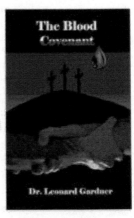

Bread that Satisfies

Are you truly satisfied in life? Is your appetite for God everything you desire it to be? The aroma of freshly baked homemade bread awakens hunger in almost anyone. Learn how to stir a similar spiritual hunger in your heart for Jesus, the Bread of Life. Knowing Him will satisfy the deepest hunger of your spirit.

PO Box 380291
Clinton Township, MI 48038
Phone: (586) 216-3668
Fax: (586) 416-4658
lgardner@liberatingword.org

Liberating
Word
Ministries

www.liberatingword.org